Living in the Blessed Place

BISHOP TIMOTHY J. CLARKE

WESTBOW
PRESS
A DIVISION OF THOMAS NELSON

WestBow Press books may be ordered through booksellers or by contacting:

WestBow Press
A Division of Thomas Nelson
1663 Liberty Drive
Bloomington, IN 47403
www.westbowpress.com
1-(866) 928-1240

ISBN: 978-1-4908-0673-0 (sc)
ISBN: 978-1-4908-0672-3 (hc)
ISBN: 978-1-4908-0674-7 (e)

Library of Congress Control Number: 2013915692

Printed in the United States of America.

WestBow Press rev. date: 9/6/2013

Author's photo: Go Pro Images
Editor: Cynthia Donaldson
Publishing Consultant: Obieray Rogers

Other Books by
Bishop Timothy J. Clarke

Caution! God at Work—Trusting God through Tough Times

Celebrating the Family: Lessons from the Book of Ruth

Making the Most of Your Time

The Price of Victory: Strategies for Winning a Faith Fight

Reclaim Your Spiritual Health

To My Sisters Beloved: A Trilogy of Encouragement

This work is dedicated to my brothers and sisters who preach.
You have inspired, encouraged, and challenged me.
Thank you!

TABLE OF CONTENTS

PART FOUR — TURNING WHERE YOU ARE INTO THE BLESSED PLACE

INTRODUCTION

There is a place in God where we move beyond a blessing to living a blessed life. It doesn't matter how old you are, how much in debt you are, or how many bad decisions you have made. If you have faith to believe God is able to reverse your situation, then you, too, can start living the blessed life in the blessed place.

The blessed place is not reserved for "super" saints or those who have been pure all of their lives. The blessed place is for people who live in the real world with real problems. We serve a God who is able to turn our mess into miracles. You may think it can't be that simple or easy, but it is. God has the power and He is no respecter of person; however, He is a respecter of faith. And wherever God sees faith, He steps in, moves, and performs a miracle.

We don't like to talk about living in the blessed place because a few preachers have misused, misquoted, and misrepresented this teaching. We have stayed away from it lest we become lumped in with them. This is a trick of the devil. Just because some people abuse the teaching doesn't stop it from being true. When we fail to preach it, and then fail to live it, we deny the saints a powerful part of their inheritance as sons and daughters of God. The Bible says, "My people are destroyed from lack of knowledge" (Hosea 4:6).

It is not the will of God for His people to be ignorant. We have not taught the saints the fullness of their inheritance. Saints have died never experiencing the fullness of life that God says they can have through Jesus Christ by the Holy Spirit. We have put them in a spiritual straightjacket. Jesus came to give us life and that more abundantly. We are to enjoy our salvation. It is God's will to bless us; and when we don't walk in those blessings, we live short of God's best for us.

I once heard a story of what might happen to us when we get to heaven. According to the story, God will show us all the things that could and should have been ours; yet, we never believed nor asked for them. Now I know that story is not a biblical truth, but it helps to point out how far below our potential we often live.

Perhaps because of our background, we tend to think that if we ask God for too much, we will bankrupt Him and heaven. We will never out-dream or out-do God in His abundance, provision, and desire to bless us. What God told Abram is what He says to us, "I will give you as far as you can see." God sees us *Living in the Blessed Place!*

PART ONE

—

GOD SAYS, "IT'S YOURS!"

CHAPTER ONE

—

God Gave Us Dominion

Many Christians are living beneath their privilege and potential. I believe this has happened because we have never been taught our original intent, purpose, or design. In other words, most people don't know the truth about who they are. Most people settle for less than God's best in every aspect of their lives.

In the book of Genesis we are told that when God first made man, He made them male and female. Then God said:

> "Be fruitful and multiply; fill the earth and subdue it; have dominion over the fish of the sea, over the birds of the air, and over every living thing that moves on the earth." (Genesis 1:28, NKJV)

Some people believe that only Adam was to have dominion, which would then mean that only men are to be in charge. However, that is not what the Bible says. While Adam is the responsible party and head of the family, God gave *both* Adam and Eve dominion and authority over the world in which they lived.

The plan and will of God was for us—male *and* female—to have dominion, to rule, and to exercise authority. In essence, our

3

assignment was to take over. However, some people believe that the devil has been in control since the Fall, and that we should just sit back and let him have his way with the world. That's crazy! Yes, it's true that man sinned, creation was marred, and Satan usurped a place of authority. But, it's equally true that God's command and plan didn't change with the entry of sin into the world. In fact, the plan of God was enlarged to now include our dominion over Satan *and* his work.

God made us to have dominion and to be in charge. Once God has said something, He will never change His mind. Please don't buy into the faulty theology that if you act up, you will throw God off base, leaving Him wringing His hands because you did something wrong. Stop flattering yourself. You are not so big that you can frustrate the plans of Almighty God. Do you think your little mistakes or failures are really going to stop God's plans? If God decides to do something, He is still enough God to do it by Himself, even if nobody cooperates. What He speaks will come to pass.

The will of God does not stop because of sin. Satan came to earth and trespassed on what God had already given us, but the command of God to take over was not rendered null and void. God merely enlarged the plan; if Satan is on your property, you must take over both the property and him. You're not in charge if the devil is bossing you around; as a child of God, you should be bossing the devil around: "Ye are of God, little children, and have overcome them: because greater is He that is in you than he that is in the world" (1 John 4:4, KJV). We are to have dominion over Satan and his works.

THE SOURCE OF OUR RESOURCES

It is still God's plan that we walk in dominion and authority. The Bible is full of accounts of men and women who did just that. They lived in the world but were not bound by or subject to the powers of the world, because they had a source of resource beyond this world. When your Source doesn't come from this world, you don't have to dance to the music of the world. Your job is not your Source; your job is the resource that your Source provided. If that resource dries up, your Source has another resource. Fixed income, Social Security, and retirement are limited resources. You have a Source greater than Medicare, Social Security, or your pension fund.

Some of you can't relate to this because you're so bound by material goods. Some of you haven't praised God since September 11, 2001, because your stocks and bonds have the hiccups and your portfolio has pneumonia. All of your earnings have gone south and you're still losing money like the Titanic took on water. Your mind is on Wall Street and you're worried about your portfolio because that's your Source. I'm not going to sit around with my arms folded, refusing to give God praise. I choose to believe what David said: "I was young and now I am old, yet I have never seen the righteous forsaken or their children begging bread" (Psalm 37:25).

The men and women in the Bible enjoyed the blessings of God. Those blessings allowed them to live at another level and to experience life the way God intended. Often, we make the mistake of defining blessings too narrowly. We relegate them to material possessions only. Blessings are more than material accumulation. Blessings are gifts that come from God and represent the favor and smile of God in and on our lives. We enjoy the blessings of life, health, sound mind, wisdom, peace, joy, and salvation, to name a few. Some of you can only praise God for a new house, new car, or a raise. If you never get another house, another car, or another raise, you still have reasons to praise God: "Blessed be the Lord, Who daily loads us with benefits" (Psalm 68:19, NKJV).

People who understand their right to be blessed are ready for promotion. It took me awhile to grasp this concept because the old saints taught me to be glad I am saved, to observe all of the rules and regulations, and to live holy and godly (translate: boring); then God would let me into heaven. I was taught that I shouldn't ask for anything else. But the light bulb has finally come on and I understand that I am the righteousness of God; I am accepted in the beloved; and I have a Father who has everything. As a child of the King, what would I look like walking around poor, broke, busted, and disgusted? That doesn't bring glory to my Father. My Father looks good when His offspring look good.

As believers, we have a right to live in the blessed place. That right was purchased by what Jesus did on Calvary. If you're ready to get to the place where God's blessings are real in your life, then keep reading.

CHAPTER TWO

—

A Covenant Relationship

Every now and then God will bypass the people who think they should be chosen and He will put His hand on you. He will save, anoint, gift, deliver, forgive, bless, and prosper you.

Abram (Abraham) is a model of a man who knew about living in a blessed place. When we are first introduced to Abram, he is not a believer; he is a heathen and an idol worshipper, but God chose him anyway:

> The Lord had said to Abram, "Go from your country, your people and your father's household to the land I will show you." (Genesis 12:1)

The way Abram came to the place of blessing is the way that we, too, will come to ours. God's challenge to Abram was to get up, to leave, and to step out:

> So Abram went, as the Lord had told him; and Lot went with him. Abram was seventy-five years old when he set out from Haran. He took his wife Sarai, his nephew Lot, all the possessions

they had accumulated and the people they had acquired in Haran, and they set out for the land of Canaan, and they arrived there. (Genesis 12:4-5)

A PARTIAL YES IS STILL A NO

We can never experience God's best until we are willing to walk in obedience. A lot of people have a Saul mentality and they think it is okay to only do part of what God says:

> ". . .I will punish the Amalekites for what they did to Israel when they waylaid them as they came up from Egypt. Now go, attack the Amalekites and totally destroy all that belongs to them. Do not spare them; put to death men and women, children and infants, cattle and sheep, camels and donkeys." (1 Samuel 15:2-3)

In spite of God's very clear instructions, Saul chose to spare the king and the best of the sheep, cattle, fattened calves, and lambs. When questioned by Samuel as to why he hadn't obeyed the Lord, Saul said:

> "But I did obey the Lord. I went on the mission the Lord assigned me. I completely destroyed the Amalekites and brought back Agag their king. The soldiers took sheep and cattle from the plunder, the best of what was devoted to God, in order to sacrifice them to the Lord your God at Gilgal." (1 Samuel 15:20-21)

God was not impressed with Saul's explanation and told him, through Samuel, that to obey is better than to sacrifice. God says the same thing to us. Obedience is about our hearts. Obedience means that whatever God says, asks, or requires, our answer is an immediate yes. Obedience must be the standard at every level of our lives and include everything we have (time, talent, treasure), especially since all that we have comes from God. We need to fully understand and accept this. We don't own anything. We are only stewards of what God owns. Even your breath is not your own, because if God withdrew breath from you, you would fall like a sack of potatoes. Your life is in God's hand:

- Your time belongs to God. If God says get involved in a ministry, don't tell Him no. When you tell God you don't have time, He will rearrange your time. That's why some of you have the latest devices with all the bells and whistles and you are still disorganized. If you give God your time, He will stretch it.

- Your talent belongs to God. If God says use your special talent to do something, don't tell Him no. He has given you whatever talent you have and you should share it.

- Your treasure belongs to God. If God wants you to give, don't tell Him no, like you don't have the money. If you don't give it to God, you won't enjoy it. Your furnace will break down, your dryer will go out, or your car engine will blow up.

A WORD AND A PROMISE

When Abram left Haran, he had no map, no navigational system on his donkey, and no designated destination. The only thing Abram had was a Word from God and a promise; but because that Word and promise came from God, he could boldly step out and stand on them. You can, too.

Some of us are too smart for our own good. God tells us

something He wants us to do. We take out our laptop, surf the net, download all the information, create graphs and charts, print them out, give God the presentation, lay it out before Him and say, "Now based on this, this, and this, what you said can't happen. I have researched it and studied it. I have looked into this and investigated that. Based on the prevailing trends in the economy, there is no way I can do this. Stocks are down, money is tight, and the economy is on life support. Once things settle down, I'll take up your proposal." That's what so-called smart people do.

On the other hand, people of faith say, "What did you say, God? You said I can do this? Okay, let's go! I don't know where the money is coming from, but you said to do it, so I'm going to do it."

There's a story told of a rural county that was experiencing a drought. Somebody got an idea to pray for rain and everybody marched to church on Monday night. They went past the home of the chairman of the deacon board and asked him if he was coming. He said, "Maybe," but didn't show up that night or the rest of the week. Finally, the committee confronted him and said, "You're the chairman of the deacon board and are supposed to be our leader. We've been out here praying for rain all week and you didn't join us. It would be one thing if we thought you were out of town, but you sat on your front porch and watched us walk to church and pray." He agreed. They then said, "You need to explain to us why you didn't come." He said, "You don't have any faith." They questioned what he was talking about since they went to church every night to pray for rain. He said, "I watched you every night, but not one of you had an umbrella, so you couldn't have believed it was going to rain. If just one of you had taken an umbrella, I would have met you at church and prayed with you. If you're going to pray for rain, get an umbrella and a raincoat."

The way to the blessed life is through faith and by taking God at His Word, even when what you have heard God say does not appear to make any sense.

THERE'S A BLESSING IN CONFESSING

In Genesis 17, Abram and Sarai received another promise about their inheritance. God said, "I'm going to make your seed more numerous than the stars in heaven and the sand of the seashore. I'm going to give you more seed than you can count. I'm going to change your name from Abram to Abraham, Father of Many Nations, and from Sarai to Sarah, Mother of Many Nations, so that every time you say each other's name, you'll confess what I said." So every time Sarah said, "Abraham, breakfast is ready," she was really saying, "Father of Many Nations, breakfast is ready." Every time Abraham said, "Sarah, are you ready to go shopping?" he was really saying, "Mother of Many Nations, are you ready to go shopping?" Every time they called each other by name, they were confessing what they believed:

> "Truly I tell you, if anyone says to this mountain, 'Go, throw yourself into the sea,' and does not doubt in their heart but believes that what they say will happen, it will be done for them."
> (Mark 11:23)

Is it possible that the reason you have what you have is because you're getting what you confess? For example, you say your husband is no good; and he isn't. You say your children are never going to be anything; and they aren't. You say the Church is dead; so when the Holy Ghost is bouncing off the walls, you sit there like a bump on a log. You say you are never going to get better; so let's plan your funeral now. If you say you can't get out of the hole and will always be in a rut, then you'll be in the hole and in a rut the rest of your life. The Bible says that life and death are in the power of the tongue (Proverbs 18:21). Since the power is in my tongue, I have decided to change my language; I'm saying:

- "I'm blessed and everybody around me is blessed."
- "I can't go under, I'm going over."
- "I shall live and not die because the Lord is on my side."
- "I'm blessed in the city and in the field; my basket and my store are blessed."
- "I'm on my way to a blessed place."

Start confessing that your family is saved, your marriage is healed, your mind is clear, your spirit is revived, and your money is coming. You're blessed! Choose to believe the report of the Lord that says you're healed, blessed, and delivered. Start today confessing and believing what you want. You can speak to dead situations and they'll come to life. You can speak to negative situations and God will turn them around.

If you need a blessing from God, or for Him to do something supernatural in your life, then remember that the way to the blessed life is through positive confession.

CHAPTER THREE

—

Power To Get Wealth

Deuteronomy 8:18 (NKJV) says:

> "And you shall remember the Lord your God, for
> it is He who gives you power to get wealth, that
> He may establish His covenant which He swore
> to your fathers, as it is this day."

The word *power* means the ability, the authority, and the right to get wealth. We have never been taught that we have the right to expect success. Instead, we have been taught to be surprised when we succeed, which is why anyone who succeeds ends up on the cover of a magazine; we make them a celebrity. We have never been taught that you can expect to be blessed simply because you're a child of God.

God gives us the ability to get wealth, so that He can establish the same covenant with us that He made with Abram:

> "I will make you into a great nation, and I will
> bless you; I will make your name great, and you
> will be a blessing. I will bless those who bless

you, and whoever curses you I will curse; and all peoples on earth will be blessed through you." (Genesis 12:2-3)

When God spoke, the Word exited His mouth and entered the atmosphere. Since that time God has been following that Word around to accomplish it. All God is looking for is somebody who believes the Word, who believes the report of God, and who will claim his or her rights. The moment He finds that person, He establishes the covenant He made with Abram. He says, "I am going to make you wealthy by giving you what I promised Abram. If I give you what I promised Abram, money won't excite you because I'm going to give you what money can't buy. I will give you my favor, and my favor will do what your money could never do." Everything God promised Abram is for us.

THE PURPOSE OF THE ANOINTING

There are many believers who have never been taught how to walk in their blessing or their anointing. Whenever we talk about walking in our blessing, it is imperative that we understand that the only way we can do this is by understanding the purpose of the anointing. Vital to getting to a blessed place is our understanding the function of unction in our lives. God anoints us, not only to minister and serve, but also to experience and walk in everything He has for us.

Sometimes we make spiritual truths so deep that the average believer never realizes that the anointing is for them. The average believer is convinced that as long as the pastor is anointed, then everything is all right. The anointing is not just for a select few in the Church; the anointing is for every believer. As a believer in Christ, you have the right to walk in your anointing. The purpose of your anointing is to move you into the place where God wants you to be. The anointing is the hand, power, and favor of God on your life. We all have natural abilities, wisdom, and knowledge. When the anointing is added, you are no longer operating in the natural, but in the supernatural. A simple way of describing the anointing is to say that the anointing is God's *super* on your *natural*, and what you would have done in the flesh is magnified and enhanced. Isn't that what you want? You don't want flesh on display. After fighting the devil all week long, you want to sit under anointed ministers. But, the anointing is not just for Sunday morning. The anointing covers every area of your life, every day of your life:

> "And you shall remember the Lord your God, for it is He who gives you power to get wealth that He may establish His covenant which He swore to your fathers, as it is this day." (Deuteronomy 8:18, NKJV)

Most people focus on the word *wealth* instead of the word *power.* Wealth is a by-product of power. Power helps you get wealth. Power not only means ability, authority, and the right; it also means anointing. It is the Lord thy God who anoints you to get wealth.

The same anointing that I have to preach is on me to get wealth. Whatever anointing is on your life is the same anointing to get wealth. You have a right to be wealthy. You have a right to be blessed.

It is the Lord thy God who has anointed you to have power to get wealth so that He might fulfill His covenant in you. It is the will of God to take you to a blessed place. When you walk under the anointing, you will experience certain things that come your way as a result of the favor of God.

CHAPTER FOUR

—

Total Blessings

In Genesis chapter 12, Abram received a Word and a promise from God that revealed His plan and intention to bless Abram. Later portions of the story show how God's plan included the totality of his life and being. According to the promise, Abram was to be blessed financially, physically, spiritually, and relationally. It was to be a total blessing.

Some people think the only blessing we get from God involves money. If the only barometer for blessing is the size of our bank account, then what we preach about God isn't true: "..... of a truth I perceive that God is no respecter of persons" (Acts 10:34, KJV). There are godly people in third world countries who don't have a bank account. If driving a new car is the only way I can say I'm blessed, then what does God say about the preacher in Africa who rides a bicycle thirty miles to preach the gospel? He's faithful, too. God's blessings are not limited to what's in your pocket; His blessings cover your heart, your mind, and your life.

Some of you may be able to relate to the fact that some of your greatest blessings had nothing to do with money. Perhaps your child got saved; or someone you loved was at the point of death and God brought him back; or you almost sinned but God stepped in and shielded you in the hour of temptation. You can't put a price tag on this. Every time you wake up in the morning, God has already blessed you; and all day long He is showering you with blessings.

Bruce Wilkinson says in the *Prayer of Jabez* that when Jabez prayed, "O, that you would bless me indeed," he was actually saying, "God, I want you to bless me a lot," or "Give me a total blessing." That is what God did for Abram; and I'm convinced that this is what God wants to do for us. If we are honest, the vast majority of us don't believe that God wants to bless us; and we don't know what to do with blessings once we get them. In fact, most of us don't recognize blessings when they come; thus, we waste them, ignore them, and lose them. So, what do you do with blessings from God?

RECEIVE YOUR BLESSINGS

When God told Abram that He was going to bless him, Abram never asked, "Why me, Lord?" or said, "No God, I'm not worthy." He simply received what God wanted to give him. This is where most Christians struggle. We say we want blessings but I'm convinced that there are blessings we could have had but we didn't know how to receive them. Our struggle will usually fall into one of two categories:

- I don't feel that I qualify or deserve a blessing: "I'm not good enough." "I haven't been saved long enough." "This can't possibly all be for me!"

- I don't need a blessing: "I can make it on my own." "I can handle life by myself." "I've got it all under control."

This is what makes being blessed difficult, because you have to realize that blessings have nothing to do with you. You will never be blessed because you deserve it.

One day I was praying and telling God how good I had been. The Lord reminded me about some things I had forgotten and that my righteousness was still like filthy rags. God told me, "Don't come to me in your righteousness. You don't know what you're going to do five minutes from now, so let's not get into a bragging contest." Then He said, "Whatever I have done for you, whatever I am doing in you, and whatever I am going to do for you in the future doesn't have anything to do with you and your record. It has to do with me and my grace."

We want to drag our record to God, tell Him how good we are, and then believe that He has to bless us. We never deserve the blessings of God. All we can do is throw ourselves on the mercy of God and trust that He loves us enough to supply our needs and do what's best for us. We don't deserve to be blessed. We can't earn it. It isn't even because we need it. We are blessed because God decides to bless us. And sometimes He doesn't just give us what we need; He will open up the windows of heaven and give us what we want. We can live in the overflow and have more than enough:

> "Bring the whole tithe into the storehouse, that there may be food in my house. Test me in this," says the Lord Almighty, "and see if I will not throw open the floodgates of heaven and pour out so much blessing that there will not be room enough to store it." (Malachi 3:10)

God doesn't just give us what we need; every now and then He will pour out more because of His favor. There comes a point when we can stop walking in God's blessing and start walking in His favor. When you walk in His favor, outrageously good things begin to happen. People start blessing you for no reason. When you're in God's favor, you are getting things that have been stored up for your lean times. God saw you when you couldn't get a break; when you couldn't see your way; and when you didn't have two nickels to rub together—and you praised Him anyhow. God was keeping a record and now you're in your season. When God begins to bless you, He does it without measure. When God is ready to bless you, you must first receive it. Don't offer false modesty. Receive the blessing and know that God is paying you back for something.

Do you understand that most of the blessings you're enjoying are the favor of God? You have a job you weren't trained to do. You're driving a car that your credit report says you can't afford. You're living in a house beyond your means. You're dressing better than the money you have in your pocket. God is there opening up doors and making a way for you; He causes people to bless you. God sends unexpected advantages into our lives not because we've earned them or deserve them, but because of His favor. So, what do blessings require?

- Blessings require dependence. In order to receive a blessing, you have to realize that you're dependent on God.

- Blessings require humility. Don't get arrogant about your blessings. You can't walk around with your nose in the air because you've been blessed.

- Blessings require gratitude. When you've been blessed, tell God "Thank You" and worship and praise Him for what He has done for you.

MODEL YOUR BLESSINGS

God does some things for the sake of His holy name and His glory. When God brought Israel out of Egypt, it was for His glory, so Pharaoh and the world would know that He is God. When God blesses us, it's not just to give us something; it's to let the world see the goodness and greatness of our God.

When you are blessed by God, one of the things you have to do is model your blessing. People know you couldn't have pulled it off on your own, so the only thing they can say is, "Look what God has done." A lot of saints have been blessed and are hiding it. You're keeping your blessings hidden because you're afraid of what other saints are going to say. You're afraid they'll think you're showing off or bragging. The people you're worried about are the "ain'ts," not the saints. The saints will rejoice with you; the ain'ts will be the ones who say you're bragging, showing off, or thinking you're better than everybody else. Saints are not threatened when other saints get a new car, new house, promotions, or any other blessing from the Lord. Saints understand that it may be your turn today, but it might be their turn tomorrow:

- Model your blessings with integrity. Get the blessing the right way. Don't model something you gained through theft or prostitution. Don't model a dress or drive a car you purchased with God's tithe. If you're going to model blessings, have integrity.

- Model your blessings with confidence. God has been good to you. Don't be ashamed of what you have.

- Model your blessings with boldness. Tell everybody, everywhere, that God did it!

SHARE YOUR BLESSINGS

God made it clear to Abram that he was not being blessed just for himself but for others. God does everything on purpose, with purpose, so others are blessed by and through us. We are conduits and channels, not repositories and vaults. We must not hoard or hold God's blessings. His blessings flow through us because we have an obligation to bless others. God shouldn't have to break our arm to convince us to share the blessing:

- We are to share willingly and not out of compulsion.

- We are to share joyfully and without an attitude.

- We are to share frequently. The more you give, the more God gives to you.

After you have been blessed, you should bless someone else. When you give to the poor, you're lending to the Lord: "The King will reply, 'Truly I tell you, whatever you did for one of the least of these brothers and sisters of mine, you did for me'" (Matthew 25:40).

CHAPTER FIVE

—

The Promise of Blessings

God wants to abundantly supply our needs according to His riches in glory (Philippians 4:19). Nothing your mind can comprehend or imagine is too great for God. He is able to go further than you've ever dreamed possible, because He is the God of more than enough.

Some people don't want to believe God is waiting to bless them, because it shifts the responsibility back to them. It's hard to believe that some people are comfortable in poverty and believe waiting for a welfare check is easier than punching a time clock at a job. But when you are dependent upon other people, they are empowered to dictate and determine your life. They tell you how much you can have and what to do with your money. You must come to a place of maturity where you decide you're only going to depend on God as your Source.

When you live in prosperity, you won't be willing to wait for anybody to provide a handout,. You'll get up in the morning and trust God that as you go about your day, He will give you favor, open up doors, and send promotion. When God gets ready to bless you, no one can stop it. When God gets ready to promote you, no one can pull you down: "The blessings of

the LORD makes one rich, And He adds no sorrow with it"
(Proverbs 10:22, NKJV).

When God made a covenant with Abram, it was not a one-
time, one-person, one-generation blessing.

I AM GOING TO BLESS YOU AND
MAKE YOUR NAME GREAT

Critics of Bruce Wilkinson's book the *Prayer of Jabez* say that
there's too much "me" in his prayer. "O, that thou would bless
me indeed; keep your hand upon *me*." We do have to be cautious
that we don't become obsessed with "me-ism." But Dr. Wilkinson
makes a salient point: "When Jabez prays, 'O, that thou would
bless me indeed,' he is not being selfish; he's being honest." I
agree and here's why: If I'm not blessed, I can't bless anybody
else. Sometimes I have to make it personal and pray, "God bless
me. And after you bless me, help me to remember that you didn't
bless me just to be blessed. You blessed me to help somebody else."

All I am trying to tell you is don't get upset because God is
blessing somebody near you or connected to you. If somebody close
to you is getting blessed, just hang around. It won't be long before
they bless you or God decides to put you at the head of the blessing
line. That's why you should want your pastor to be blessed. I wouldn't
want to sit under a leader who wasn't blessed. What can they tell you
about being blessed if they aren't blessed? If you are a leader who is
being blessed, then the people under your leadership should be like
a saucer that catches the overflow from the cup. As our leaders get
blessed, the people who follow them should also be blessed.

I AM GOING TO BLESS YOUR SEED AFTER YOU

I once heard a preacher speak of fathers blessing their sons and
daughters and shooting them like arrows into the future. It's
important for our children to have the blessing of their fathers.

Our children go through a lot of things because they never get blessed. I'm not saying that they never get stuff; it's just that they never get blessed. There is a blessing that a father gives his children that nobody else can give. As a father, I must bless and speak good things over my children.

I also have to bless my spiritual sons and daughters. There are some things that my natural children get as my biological seed, but my spiritual seed should get something, too. They are to do ministry at a higher level than me. When I shoot them into the future, I expect them to build ministries that are greater than my own; and they should do it quicker than I did because I have already laid the foundation. Those anointed to pastoral ministry should pastor churches with thousands and should get there quicker than I did. The seed always gets more than the first generation.

Unfortunately, a lot of preachers don't want to share their blessing. If I'm anointed, I have been anointed to pass it on to somebody else. My spiritual fathers never had churches as large as First Church; I have accomplished what they were never able to do, and well I should. My spiritual children should do even better than I have; and I see no reason to be jealous.

God told Abram that He was going to bless him; He knew that Abram would be unable to bless anybody else until he received the blessing. And then God told Abram that He was going to bless his seed.

I AM GOING TO BLESS ALL THE NATIONS OF THE EARTH THROUGH YOU

The blessing was never meant to stop, cease, or end. In fact, the blessing was extended and expanded, in Christ; and we are heirs to the promise and the blessing. Abram's covenant with God was good, but we have an even better one. We have Abram's covenant coupled with a new covenant, which is signed with the blood of Jesus Christ.

Some of you may think the call of Abram sounds like God was promising him a one-time blessing. In fact when you read the covenants that God made with him, they always included his offspring, his seed, and his future. Long after Abram was dead, his seed and offspring were continually blessed. It is not a sign of the favor of God for you to be blessed and your children, grandchildren, and great-grandchildren to be broke. If you are blessed and walking in favor, then your offspring should be more blessed than you. Every generation should get the compound interest of the blessing in which you're walking.

One of the most atrocious signs I have ever seen appeared on a bumper sticker; it read, "I am spending my children's inheritance." It may sound cute, but it's not biblical. The Bible says "A good man leaves an inheritance for his children's children" (Proverbs 13:22, NKJV). If I walk in favor, my great-grandchildren should have more favor than me. It's not enough that I walk in blessings. The real blessings of God extend to the generations following us.

I believe we should leave money for our children and grandchildren; but as Christians, we also have an obligation to leave some of our money for the advancement of the Kingdom. If you love God, the Kingdom, and the Church, your last will and testament should reflect your love. The saints who love God and serve Him faithfully should give careful thought to how their money will be distributed once they die; it doesn't make sense for the saints to leave all of their money to unsaved relatives and heathens who will waste it on worldly pursuits, while the Kingdom of God goes without. If people can leave money to hospitals, Masonic organizations, their pets, and anything else, then the saints of God should leave some money for building up the Kingdom and the Church.

I'm not asking you to do something I haven't done. My wife and I have already decided to leave money to the Church we've served for over thirty years. What would it look like for me to give leadership to First Church of God, the Church that I say I love, and then fail to mention it anywhere in my will? Jesus said that your treasure will be where your heart is. If you don't leave anything to the Church, I have to wonder if you ever loved the Church.

Abram was a blessing to the world. God told him, "In you every family of the earth will be blessed." That's the job of the Church. The Church doesn't just exist to luxuriate in its own self-indulgence:

> "You are the salt of the earth; but if the salt loses its flavor, how shall it be seasoned? It is then good for nothing but to be thrown out and trampled underfoot by men. You are the light of the world. A city that is set on a hill cannot be hidden." (Matthew 5:13-14, NKJV)

Our job is to touch the world with the gospel of Jesus Christ, but you can't do that without resources and money. There are some things that take more than prayer alone. You can pray for people with AIDS, but it takes money to build a house where they can live and die with dignity. Our senior citizens need housing in their twilight years; shouting isn't going to build the house.

Contrast the experience of Abram with the experiences you and I have in being blessed. Most of us can look back and see places where we received a blessing. If we are honest, we will admit that we prayed, fasted, and consecrated ourselves to get the blessing. And now that we're weeks, months, years removed from that particular blessing, there is no evidence of the blessing. We did all that praying, fasting, and consecrating for a car, a house, a raise, a promotion, or some extra money. Now it's all gone, and you can't remember anything you did with the money you received.

Blessings are not things. Blessings come with and from God, and are evidence of the favor, power, and anointing of God in your life. That's more than a one-time hit on the blessing machine.

PART TWO

—

CHALLENGES ALONG THE WAY

CHAPTER SIX

—

Moving to the Blessed Place

God wants to establish a covenant with you to fulfill the promise that He made to Abram:

> "I will make you into a great nation, and I will bless you; I will make your name great, and you will be a blessing. I will bless those who bless you and whoever curses you I will curse; and all peoples on earth will be blessed through you." (Genesis 12:2-3)

This is where God wants us to live; but the tragedy is that rather than pressing into the blessed place, some of us are settling for a blessing. A blessing is good, but why fast and pray to just get a blessing? The devil has made us content with a blessing, when God has said He wants to move us from a blessing to living in a blessed place.

One of the things I see happening in the Church today is a lot of emphasis on getting a blessing. We have turned God into a spiritual slot machine where we put in a seed (an offering or a gift) and then pull the lever and hope for a windfall. That is a perversion of how God operates, and it's a sign of how carnal the Church has become. Blessings are not chances. We are not gambling or betting on God when we give or plant a seed of faith. We were so comfortable gambling in our former life; now we have come into the Kingdom and we're treating God like our bookie. We give, sow a seed, pay our tithe, and cross our fingers hoping that we're going to get a blessing. When we give to God, we are not gambling, betting, or taking a chance. Mature saints will testify that when you pay your tithe or give an offering, you're really paying for blessings that you have already received. God has been good to you. He has kept you from dangers seen and unseen. He has provided for you. He has made a way for you. He has fought battles for you. He has preserved and protected your life from the onslaught of the enemy. God has already done more than you deserve.

A lot of us aren't walking in this truth because we don't believe it. Or, we believe it for others, but not for ourselves. Understand this: You have to stop thinking that others have a right to something but you don't. Why do you think God won't bless you?

Another reason we're not walking in this truth is because we don't understand it. We look for a blessing rather than a blessed place. We think all blessings are material, which is only a small part of how God blesses us. Material blessings are something you have, whereas spiritual, emotional, and mental blessings are something that you are.

The will of God is not to give us a blessing here and there or every now and then; His will is to bring us to a blessed place where we live out our right to be blessed. We're in covenant with God through Jesus Christ. God wants this relationship with us because He knows the power of blessings and what they do in our lives. We change when we walk in our blessing. How would you act if all your bills were paid, all your needs were met, and all your debts were settled? You would be strutting around like a peacock. Blessed people act differently because they know who they are and act accordingly. Knowing who you are doesn't just change your circumstances; it changes you.

If you settle for a blessing, you'll act a certain way as long as the blessing is operative. As long as your car still has that new car smell, you're excited. As soon as it starts getting older, you'll change the way you act. Getting a new dress or suit is a blessing. You look and feel good; but when it starts getting old, you're no longer excited. When you're living in a blessed place, you'll put on an old dress or suit and still act like you have a million dollars. You'll drive an old car and still act like you own the world, because it's not about what's on your back or what you're driving.

God wants you to stop begging for a blessing and to start living the blessed life. When God changed Abram's name to Abraham, he didn't have any children. He and Sarah were walking around calling each other Father and Mother of Many Nations but they didn't have any children. When you've been changed, you won't let your environment dictate your response. Who you are conditions your environment.

God wants to get us to a blessed place because He wants us to live a life that the world will envy, instead of the other way around. There is something wrong when the people in the Church look lustfully at the world, because the world is living large and we are barely surviving. It should be the other way around. The world should look at the Church and say, "I don't understand how they're able to do what they do. They only have a little bit of money and the people are not all that well off. It seems as if they have help that isn't natural." We then confirm it's true, we do have help that's not natural because our help comes from the Lord. We are God's ambassadors and we should look the part.

LIVING IN A BLESSED PLACE
REMOVES COMPETITION

We must realize that when we are blessed, it's not because we're so wonderful. Other saints have been just as faithful and they are still waiting on their blessing:

"Be careful not to practice your righteousness in front of others, to be seen by them. If you do, you will have no reward from your Father in heaven. So when you give to the needy, do not announce it with trumpets, as the hypocrites do in the synagogues and on the streets, to be honored by others." (Matthew 6:1-2)

The blessed place removes competition because the mindset at the heart of competition believes that I have to win and be the top dog. In the blessed place I am not competing with anyone to see who can get the biggest, fastest blessing. What God has for me is for me.

LIVING IN A BLESSED PLACE REMOVES JEALOUSY

When I know that God is taking care of me and handling my business, I don't have to be jealous of anyone else:

"Therefore I tell you, do not worry about your life, what you will eat or drink; or about your body, what you will wear. Is not life more than food, and the body more than clothes? Look at the birds of the air; they do not sow or reap or store away in barns, and yet your heavenly Father feeds them. Are you not much more valuable than they?" (Matthew 6:25-26)

Once I move into a blessed place, I have no reason to be jealous. We are only jealous of what others have when we think we have no hope of getting the same thing. Think about it. You're not jealous of the other people on your job who get paid, because you get paid, too. You aren't jealous of a person who has a car, if you have a car. Jealousy only kicks in when the devil says you will never get what somebody else has. That's why God wants to get you into a blessed place. Blessed people are never jealous because they say, "It might be your turn today, but if I'm faithful and wait on God, it may be my turn tomorrow." You don't have to be jealous when you know your blessing is coming. God wants you to stop begging for blessings and to start living in the blessed place.

LIVING IN A BLESSED PLACE REMOVES WORRY

Jesus knows what you need and will take care of you:

> "And why do you worry about clothes? See how the flowers of the field grow. They do not labor or spin. Yet I tell you that not even Solomon in all his splendor was dressed like one of these. If that is how God clothes the grass of the field, which is here today and tomorrow is thrown into the fire, will he not much more clothe you—you of little faith?" (Matthew 6:28-30)

Jesus is saying, "If you have me, what are you worried about? If I take care of sparrows and feed them; if I take care of flowers and clothe them, can't you trust me to take care of you? I know what you need and I will take care of you."

When we live in a blessed place, we should be worry-free. That doesn't mean there are no challenges, struggles, or opposition. As a matter of fact, one of the signs of being in the blessed place is challenge, struggle, and opposition. But, please don't just settle for a blessing; press into the blessed place.

CHAPTER SEVEN

—

The Blessing of Adversity

For the past few chapters you have been reading about the place and power of blessings in your life. Now I want to examine a subject that may seem contradictory, but it's a truth we need to fully understand if we are serious about moving to a blessed place.

It's not enough for me to tell you that God wants to bless you; you need a strategy for moving to a blessed place, and that's what I'm trying to provide. It's one thing to get inspired, and it's something else to have the tools to implement your inspiration. We tell people what to do, but we don't tell them how to do it. We tell people what they should have, but we never tell them how to get it. I don't want to tell you that you're blessed; I want to help you get to where God is trying to take you. Although I have been talking about blessings and prosperity, I now want to talk about the flip side of prosperity; namely, adversity. I want to suggest that there is a blessing in adversity. When we run from struggles or try to avoid pain, we may be missing the very thing that leads us to our blessed place:

> "And we know that in all things God works for the good of those who love Him, who have been called according to His purpose." (Romans 8:28)

34

If you will embrace this truth, then it won't be difficult to accept what you're about to read. If Romans 8:28 is true, then nothing we encounter (job layoffs, disobedient children, wayward spouses, or condescending saints) is outside of God's power and ability to make it work for our good.

The Bible reveals that all of the well-known biblical personalities who were used, blessed, and favored by God went through adversity: Moses spent 40 years in the desert; Israel wandered the wilderness for 40 years; Joseph was wrongfully imprisoned; David escaped Saul's murder attempts; Jesus suffered in Gethsemane and on Calvary; and Paul spent years in jail fighting for justice.

We like to read the book of Revelation where John saw Jesus high and lifted up, and with a voice like the sound of water; but we forget that John was in a jungle on the Isle of Patmos. If there had not been a Patmos, John wouldn't have had a revelation. Paul and Silas were praying and singing and the jail shook. They had to be in jail for the jail to shake. We like to shout about the love of Jesus, but He proved His love by going to the cross.

The way to the blessed place is not through ease and pleasure. No cross, no crown. No grief, no glory. No pain, no gain. What holds us up and gives us hope is that while we're going through, we have Romans chapter 8.

God knows where we are and what we're going through:

> "For those God foreknew He also predestined to
> be conformed to the likeness of His Son, that He
> might be the firstborn among many brothers and
> sisters." (Romans 8:29)

Paul is reminding us that God knows everything about your life; there are no secrets. He didn't just find out this morning. Nothing happens by chance or whim. Our Sovereign God already foreknew and predestined your outcome.

Nothing can come between God and you:

> "Who shall separate us from the love of Christ?
> Shall trouble or hardship or persecution or
> famine or nakedness or danger or sword?"
> (Romans 8:35)

Nothing can separate you from God. You are still in His hand, the apple of His eye, and the object of His affection. No matter what you're going through, God is with you. Life, the devil, or people cannot separate you from God. People will try to stop, destroy, and hurt you; but they can't affect the relationship between God and you. There's nothing anybody can tell God about you that will make Him turn away from you. He has chosen to love you.

God has promised victory:

> "No, in all these things we are more than conquer-
> ors through Him who loved us." (Romans 8:37)

You need to shout on the word *"more."* How do you "more than conquer?" If you've conquered, you've conquered. If I'm in a race and I beat you, the race is over and I've won. How do I win more? God doesn't just let you get to the finish line; He doesn't just let you make it. He lets you make it with strength to spare. In Jesus Christ I'm not a winner; I'm *more* than a winner.

ENJOY THE JOURNEY

Sometimes on the road to the blessed place, we become more obsessed with the destination and miss the journey. Adversity does something for us on our way to the blessed place.

Remember the story of the man who wanted Jesus to heal his servant? The man told Jesus to just speak the word and the servant would be healed. The Bible says that "as he went," his servant was healed, which means that by the time the man arrived home, the healing was already done (Matthew 8:5-13).

If I can show you how to enjoy the benefits of the journey, you will be able to appreciate your destination once you get there. Most of us act so nasty, ugly, mean, and bitter on the way to the destination that when we finally arrive, there's no one to celebrate with because we've ostracized everyone.

Adversity trains us

Athletes know that the purpose of training is to condition, prepare, and strengthen. Because God foreknew you and predetermined your destiny, He knows where you're going and what it will take to get you there. He puts you in training and the training conditions you for the fight:

> "No discipline seems pleasant at the time, but painful. Later on, however, it produces a harvest of righteousness and peace for those who have been trained by it." (Hebrews 12:11)

I once watched a championship boxing match where George Foreman was one of the commentators. He pointed out that one of the boxers had never been able to go beyond the ninth round. Mr. Foreman further stated that if this boxer could go beyond the ninth round, that would mean that his training and conditioning had paid off.

When you're in a championship fight, you're going to experience things you have never dealt with before. You must have something in you that will give you stamina and endurance past the early rounds. Some of you can do rounds one through nine standing on one foot, with one hand tied behind your back; but God is getting ready to take you to a blessed place where you will have new demons, new oppositions, and new struggles. You're going to need strength you've never needed before. Stop fussing and complaining; stay in training.

Adversity tests us

Adversity comes into your life as a test. The purpose of a test is to determine where you are, what you know, and where you need improvement. God sends some struggles into your life to test you. It's easy to praise God when your bills are paid, your spouse is acting right, and your children are well-behaved. But, your praise on the mountain is authenticated by your praise in the valley. If you can't praise God in the valley, then your praise on the mountain doesn't really mean anything. Anybody can praise God when everything is going well, but you have to be able to praise Him when everything appears to be going wrong.

Keep in mind that what you're going through is only a test. Had it been a real test, you would have lost your mind. Had it been a real test, you would have backslid. Had it been a real test, the devil would have had you. This is only a test so you can see where you are, determine what you know, and see where you need improvement.

Adversity gives us a testimony

There is a difference between a *testimony* and a *testiphony*. When you give a testiphony, you just repeat what you heard somebody else say about God. You can't really tell us what God is doing for you because you haven't been through anything; and the reason you haven't been through anything is because you're not willing to suffer. You have never understood, there cannot be a testimony without a test. You have to be tested, so that you will know that your testimony is real.

Job said, "I know that my redeemer lives" (Job 19:25). Paul

said, ". . .because I know whom I have believed, and am convinced that He is able to guard what I have entrusted to him until that day" (2 Timothy 1:12). But that's Job and Paul. You need something of your own, and Romans 8:28 says, "We know." That's your testimony. *I know* that He is able to save you because He saved me. *I know* that He is able to keep you, because He is keeping me. *I know* He is able to make a way out of no way, because He has made a way in my life.

Getting to the blessed place is through adversity. What are you going to shout about if you haven't been through anything?

CHAPTER EIGHT

—

The Blessing of Prosperity

The book of Philippians is one of the most interesting and unusual books in the Bible. When you read Paul's letter to the churches at Philippi, you get the feeling that there is a contrast that doesn't make sense to the natural mind.

Those of you familiar with biblical composition know that this letter falls into the category known as the prison epistles, which means that Paul wrote this letter while in prison. Yet, from prison, Paul writes about joy and contentment. He was in jail, but full of joy. He was in prison, but filled with praise. He was behind bars, but counting his blessings. Paul lets us know that if we can't praise God in the bad times, then our praise in the good times really doesn't amount to much. All of us can praise God when our body is healthy. All of us can praise God when everything is peaches and cream. But can you still praise God when things turn from bad to worse—when it looks like the bottom has dropped out and the roof has caved in? If your response is yes, then you know you have a real praise. Praise doesn't just work on the mountain; real praise works down in the valley.

The book of Philippians has a lot to teach us about handling what life brings our way. It has something to teach us about living in our blessings. This is the book we should consider when moving into the blessed life.

BLESSINGS ARE MORE THAN MATERIAL THINGS

Paul could shout in his jail cell because he had something that money could not buy, prison could not contain, and jail could not take away. When we think that the only blessings of God are material in nature, we are putting our hope and faith in things that are transitory and temporary:

> "Do not store up for yourselves treasures on earth, where moths and vermin destroy, and where thieves break in and steal. But store up for yourselves treasures in heaven, where moths and vermin do not destroy, and where thieves do not break in and steal. For where your treasure is, there your heart will be also." (Matthew 6:19-21)

If you build all your hopes on the car you drive, the house you live in, and the clothes you wear, you don't understand that inflation, recession, and depression can take away your car, your house, and your clothes. If you have something on the inside, then you can lose all of your stuff and still have joy.

Paul understood that blessings are more than material things. When you're between a rock and a hard place, and you're backed up against the wall by life, you must have something that money can't buy and that life can't take away from you.

PAUL HAD JOY. Money can buy stuff, which may make you happy, but it can't buy joy. A new car will make you happy, but let somebody scratch it. Money can buy a new dress, but what happens when you gain five pounds? Joy doesn't come from what's on the outside; it comes from what's on the inside. You can praise your way out of the valley and God will give you joy in the midst of the storm.

PAUL HAD PEACE. Years ago at Moody Bible Institute, I heard the late Dr. E. V. Hill preach on the subject "What We Get When We Get Jesus." According to Dr. Hill, one of the things we get is peace. Peace is a word that is powerful and pregnant with promise. Peace is the thing we most often want and can't seem to find. Peace is not the absence of or deliverance from the storm; it is calm confidence in the midst of the storm. And at the center of peace is our relationship with God:

- Peace *with* God means I am in right relationship with Him.

- Peace *from* God enables me to handle whatever life brings my way.

- Peace *of* God is what sustains and holds me so that even in the midst of a crisis, I don't fall apart.

PAUL HAD HOPE. As a child of God, we have hope. If you have God, it doesn't matter what comes your way or what happens. If God is for you, He is more than the world against you.

DON'T RELY ON PEOPLE AS
YOUR SOURCE OF SUPPLY

There are three kinds of people in this world: those who can and won't, those who want to but can't, and those who can and will:

- Those who can and won't are selfish. They diligently hoard what they have with a mindset of "I've got mine, now go get yours."

- Those who want to but can't are just the opposite. They are basically generous by nature; however, the caution is to not allow them to waste your time. They go on and on about how much they wish they could help you.

- Those who both can and will are in the minority. They are a gift from God:

> "Moreover, as you Philippians know, in the early days of your acquaintance with the gospel, when I set out from Macedonia, not one church shared with me in the matter of giving and receiving, except you only; for even when I was in Thessalonica, you sent me aid more than once when I was in need." (Philippians 4:15-16)

Paul said even though the Philippian church had always helped (and even when they couldn't help, they had a desire to), he suggests that there were other churches that never helped.

If you put your hope and faith in people as your source of supply, you will be making a big mistake. People will yank your chain and jerk you around, if you let them. Paul teaches us the best thing to do is to put our faith in God.

ATTITUDE IS EVERYTHING

Paul chose to be joyful:

> "I am not saying this because I am in need, for I have learned to be content whatever the circumstances. I know what it is to be in need, and I know what it is to have plenty. I have learned the secret of being content in any and every situation,

whether well fed or hungry, whether living in plenty or in want." (Philippians 4:11-12)

Joy is both an action and an attitude. We choose to have it and we choose to demonstrate it. Happiness, on the other hand, is an emotion and a feeling subject to whim and will. Paul said, "I'm not happy about being in jail, but in spite of all that I have been through, I still have joy." Paul could have chosen to be depressed. If anybody had a right to sing the blues, he did. Instead, he chose to have joy.

It is this truth that leads us to the blessings of prosperity. Seeing the reason God blesses us makes what we are given even more valuable. We realize that we must be good and wise stewards of what has been given to us.

BLESSINGS ALLOW US TO FOCUS ON OUR ASSIGNMENT

God blesses us so we are able to focus on our assignment. People who are saved have a calling on their lives; we have been gifted and anointed to do an assignment. God would never call us to do something that He does not prepare and equip us to do. Your assignment is possible because He has anointed and gifted you to fulfill it.

The sad reality is that many people haven't even started on their assignment because they can't afford it. Many people are working two jobs, are in debt, and are overextended, so they can't focus on their real calling, which is to fulfill their assignment. They are controlled by the demands and dictates of their obligations. I want you to understand that going to Church on Sunday is not your only assignment. Going to Church allows you to watch preachers fulfill their assignments, but it doesn't help unless you apply what the preacher has taught you. Many of us are unhappy and unfulfilled in life, but not because God hasn't been good to us. Our spirits are restless because we know we're not doing what we were born to do. We can't afford to do our assignment and we're frustrated.

The same is true of pastors who hold dual vocations. They can't focus on their assignment, so the Church and the ministry suffer. After dual vocational pastors get through working a secular job and spending time with their families, they don't have time to pray and get a vision for their church because they have to get some sleep. God wants pastors to be blessed so we can focus on our assignment and give priority to what He has called us to do.

Allow me to pause here and to share a word with those who are dual vocational pastors or ministers. You do not have an easy task; ministry in and of itself isn't easy, and having to work forty or more hours a week only adds to the responsibility. I admire, respect, and love you. I am praying for both you and your families as you minister. Let me remind you that you matter to God and what you do in ministry matters to Him, as well. I pray that God will encourage you and I know that He will continue to bless you in every area of your life. I encourage the leaders and members to pray about making your position full time, because doing so will bless you and the Church. God is able to provide the necessary resources.

First Church of God has always taken care of me; and even when they couldn't do all they wanted to, God honored that. Since I have been free to focus on my assignment, God has grown First Church into what it is. If I had to work another job, or couldn't get paid a decent salary, or argued with my wife over money matters, my mind would not be clear enough to hear from God.

I don't want to be the only one who is blessed; I want everyone to be blessed financially, so they can focus on their assignments.

In order for everyone to focus on their assignments, we have to cooperate with God and become stewards and managers of our time, talent, and treasure. People who make a difference in this world are focused on their assignments. One of the tricks of the enemy is to get us in so much debt that we can't focus on our assignment. You're no threat to the kingdom of darkness, because you're too busy lying to and running from the bill collectors.

We have the ability to be wealthy if we would line up with what God says in His Word. Most of us can't afford to do our assignment because we owe everybody. I'm not talking about something I don't know. I haven't always been financially where I am now. I've been broke and I've been blessed, and blessed is better! I discovered some principles by getting in the Word of God and I am not broke anymore. I knew it wasn't God's will for me to be broke. God has taken me through challenges so that I can help others understand that they, too, can get beyond living hand-to-mouth. You belong to the King; and if God has it, then you should have it, too. God never intended for us to be controlled by this world's system.

God doesn't bless us so we can brag about it. God blesses us so we can focus on our assignment. We need to be free to hear from God, and that's not going to happen if we're distracted. The Church is not getting the benefit of your gifts and anointing because you're not able to focus on your assignment.

BLESSINGS ALLOW US TO WALK IN BOLDNESS

Living the blessed life gives us boldness, because we know Who is with us. Proverbs 28:1 says, "The righteous are as bold as a lion."

- Blessed people take over.

- Blessed people exercise dominion.

- Blessed people act like they have a right to rule.

One of the most wonderful things about being a pastor is the boldness it gives me. I can walk in anywhere, say what God wants me to say, turn around, and walk out. I don't have to worry about repercussions because I don't depend on outsiders to take care of me.

You have a right to rule because you are the righteousness of God. You are His seed and His child. You belong to the Most High God, the ruler of heaven and earth.

BLESSINGS ALLOW US TO LIVE WITH CONFIDENCE

Paul was in jail writing: "And my God will meet all your needs according to the riches of his glory in Christ Jesus" (Philippians 4:19). God wants you to know that you can't beat Him giving, and you can't break Him by taking. The more you give to God, the more He will give back to you. Whatever you ask for, God has that and more.

CHAPTER NINE

—

Credited to Your Account

Anyone can walk in the blessed life, because when God sees faith, He moves in and works on behalf of that person. This is the principle I want to examine in this chapter: "Not that I desire your gifts, what I desire is that more be credited to your account" (Philippians 4:17). Paul knew how to be content with what he had, so it didn't matter what someone did or didn't do. His joy was not predicated on what other people did. If they helped him, good; if they didn't, fine. Paul wasn't excited about what the Philippian church had done for him; he was excited about what their gifts would do for them. He was excited because their gifts would be credited to their account.

I'm convinced that if we understand this teaching and principle, it will revolutionize our giving. We must understand that when we give, God is not taking anything from us; He is trying to get something to us. The devil has convinced some saints that when they are asked to give an offering, their money is being taken from them. That's a lie from the pit! Giving partners you with God; and when you become His partner, all you have to do is sit back and watch Him give you more than you've given Him.

Paul was appreciative of the gifts; yet, he understood that it wasn't going to change his present circumstance—he was still in jail. But Paul determined that he was going to have joy whether they sent a gift or not. But he was excited about the return the gift would produce in their lives.

Before going any further I need to let you know that this principle is only true of a certain kind of giving. Paul said, "I am looking for the kind of gift that may be credited to your account" because not every gift gets credited. Here are the kinds of gifts that receive credit:

A willing gift

The Philippians gave because they wanted to, not because they had to:

> "I rejoiced greatly in the Lord that at last you renewed your concern for me. Indeed, you were concerned, but you had no opportunity to show it." (Philippians 4:10)

The Bible says the Lord loves a cheerful giver (2 Corinthians 9:7), which rules out about seventy percent of the saints! For many, the offering is like having a root canal without Novocain. If you give with a bad attitude, it might be better if you don't give at all. Money given with the wrong attitude does not get credited to your account. You should give willingly because that's the giving that accrues interest in your account. You'll get blessed if your attitude is right, even if you don't give as much as someone else.

Consistent giving

The Philippian church gave to Paul, even when no other church would:

"Moreover, as you Philippians know, in the early days of your acquaintance with the gospel, when I set out from Macedonia, not one church shared with me in the matter of giving and receiving, except you only; for even when I was in Thessalonica, you sent me aid more than once when I was in need." (Philippians 4:15-16)

One of the keys to being blessed is developing a faithful, consistent pattern of giving. You don't give one day and feel that you've paid your debt to God. You don't receive a blessing when you do that. There must be consistency in your giving. God honors faithful and consistent giving, even in the moments when it's apparent we cannot afford to give. If your finances are in chaos, you need to give more than anybody else. When you give, you put yourself in a position to be blessed by God. The more you need a blessing, the more you should look for opportunities to give. Giving is both an attitude and a lifestyle.

Sacrificial giving

"And my God will meet all your needs according to the riches of his glory in Christ Jesus" (Philippians 4:19). We love to quote this verse, but we miss the implication of the verse. If God is going to supply all of your needs, doesn't that presuppose there is a need? If I have everything I need, you telling me you're going to meet my need doesn't impress me. That would be like telling a billionaire you're going to give him ten dollars.

When Paul told the Philippians that God would supply all of their needs, they got excited because they realized they had a need. Giving is not really giving until it's sacrificial. Most of us have never really given. Real giving costs something and you feel the impact of having given. Matter of fact, you will know you gave because of what you have to now do without. When you drive your car another year because of what you gave, that's a sacrifice. When you decide to wear last year's dress or suit, that's a sacrifice. When you get your shoes resoled instead of buying a new pair, that's a sacrifice.

Most of us tip God. God is looking for us to give out of our need while saying, "It doesn't matter what this cost; I'm giving to the work of the Kingdom." The story of the widow's mite proves this point:

> As Jesus looked up, he saw the rich putting their gifts into the temple treasury. He also saw a poor widow put in two very small copper coins. "Truly I tell you," he said, "this poor widow has put in more than all the others. All these people gave their gifts out of their wealth; but she out of her poverty put in all she had to live on." (Luke 21:1-4)

Jesus watched all of the rich people as they gave and didn't say a word. But, when the widow brought her offering, Jesus said that she had given more than anybody because she did not give out of abundance, but out of need.

When was the last time you really gave? "For God so loved the world, that He gave His only begotten Son" (John 3:16). Jesus loves you so much, He gave His life. That's a sacrifice. What are you giving?

GOD KEEPS A RECORD

Paul was excited that gifts from the Philippian church were being credited to their account, because God keeps a record. For some of you that's good news. For others, it may be the worst news you've read this month. God has a record of everything you've given since salvation.

If God put your ledger on a screen, what would your giving

record look like? Some of you are shouting on past due credit and God is saying, it's time to get your books in order. Others may not know what your record is, but God does:

> "Do not store up for yourselves treasures on earth, where moths and vermin destroy, and where thieves break in and steal. But store up for yourselves treasures in heaven, where moths and vermin do not destroy, and where thieves do not break in and steal. For where your treasure is, there your heart will be also." (Matthew 6:19-21)

With all the talk about how much you love God, Jesus, and the Holy Ghost, will your giving record show how much you really love them? If your treasure is there, your heart will be there; and if your heart is there, your treasure will be there.

OUR GIVING WORKS FOR US LONG AFTER WE HAVE GIVEN IT

Paul said that you get a return on your giving long after you've given, because your gift keeps working for you. When you give, you don't just get an instant blessing, with God saying, "You gave to me, I gave back to you, so now we're even." If that were the case, we would all be dead. There are residual benefits that accrue based on your prior deposits.

I recently received an offer for free gifts from my credit card company, which was their way of showing appreciation for being a long-standing member. Basically what they were saying was that because I pay my bill on time, they wanted to show their gratitude and give me something unexpected and undeserved.

Every now and then when you've been faithful to God, He will say, "You didn't ask for this, but I'm going to bless you with it anyhow." You may be able to testify that what you have right now is not only because you've been faithful, but because the Lord decided to bless you. He looked at the books, saw your record, and decided to bless you with residual blessings, because what you give keeps on working long after you give it.

OUR GIVING BECOMES AN ACT OF WORSHIP

When you give an offering to the servant of God, God knows that you're really giving it to Him. It becomes a sweet smelling sacrifice, acceptable to God. When you give in the right place, with the right purpose, in the right period, God blesses everything you give. When you give, you aren't giving to people, but to the Lord. And when you give to the Lord, He will pay you back. You may already know that once you start giving, you keep getting blessed. Matter of fact, every time you turn around, God keeps on blessing you:

> "I have received full payment and have more than enough. I am amply supplied, now that I have received from Epaphroditus the gifts you sent. They are a fragrant offering, an acceptable sacrifice, pleasing to God." (Philippians 4:18)

Wait a minute, they didn't send that money to God; they sent that gift to Paul. Paul understood a basic principle of giving: When you give to a servant of God, your giving will be counted as a gift to God. Paul knew that gifts were nice, but he also knew that all of his help came from the Lord. His real blessings were intangible: His relationship with God, his peace of mind and knowing that all of his needs were met because of Jesus Christ.

"And my God shall supply all of your needs according to His riches in glory by Christ Jesus" (Philippians 4:19). Don't get so excited about the first part—"And my God shall supply all of your needs"—get excited about "according to His riches in glory." Do you have any idea just how rich God is? The cattle on a thousand hills belong to the Lord; the earth is the Lord's and the fullness thereof, the world and they that dwell therein (Psalm 50:10, Psalm 24:1). Everything you need is in the hands of God.

CHAPTER TEN

—

Trouble: A Stepping Stone to the Blessed Life

If there is a blessing in adversity, then trouble is merely another stepping stone to the blessed life. Trouble is not a hindrance to blessings; it prepares, conditions, and qualifies us to be blessed.

The devil pulls out all the stops when you are moving to your blessed place. The devil doesn't mess with you as long as you're fumbling around and don't know your head from a hole in the ground. The devil isn't thinking about you because he has bigger fish to fry. But he pulls out every stop when he sees you on the path that's taking you to your blessed place; when he knows that you're about to get to a place where he will never be able to stop you again; and when he sees you moving toward your destiny. He knows if he doesn't stop you now, it will be too late. That's why you need to stop wilting like a flower and folding up like a tent just because you hit a snag, a speed bump, or a detour.

You have sat down on God; you used to be on fire, full of zeal and excitement. Now you're sitting around depressed and dejected because you ran into trouble. Trouble is only a sign the devil believes in you more than you believe in yourself. Trouble is a sign that you are closer than you've ever been. Trouble is a compliment that says you're doing something that's giving the devil fits, making him worry that you just might get there. He has received the announcement, "We interrupt this program to bring you a special news bulletin. I think she's going to make it! I think he's going to make it! You better send for reinforcements."

If the devil is fighting you, consider it a compliment. He must know that you're close to your breakthrough. You should thank the devil because he's letting you know that you're nearer to the blessed life than ever before.

NOTHING CAN CHANGE OR ALTER WHO YOU ARE OR WHAT GOD HAS FOR YOU

The Apostle Peter wrote to Christians who had fled because of the persecution of the Church. His purpose was to encourage those under attack and to remind them that in spite of how it looked, everything was going to be all right. No matter what you're going through, there are some things the devil can't touch:

> "Blessed be the God and Father of our Lord Jesus Christ, which according to His abundant mercy hath begotten us again unto a lively hope by the resurrection of Jesus Christ from the dead, to an inheritance incorruptible, and undefiled, and that fadeth not away, reserved in heaven for you."
> (1 Peter 1:3-4, KJV)

This is like having a reservation in a restaurant. It doesn't matter that there is a line; when you arrive, you go to the head of the line because you have a reservation.

Peter said there are some things that are incorruptible, undefiled, eternal, and reserved in heaven for you. Yes, you're under attack and persecution, but you need to know there are some things the devil can't touch. He can touch your job, your money, and your possessions, but he can't touch your soul or your joy. I'm not teaching eternal security; however the devil and his imps can't change what God has said, once He decides to do something. If God has said that you're going to a blessed place, you're going; no one can keep you from what God has for you.

No matter what you're going through, you can only worry so much. When the devil came to God about Job, God told him he could touch everything Job had, but to not touch him. When the devil came the second time, God said he could touch Job's body, but not his soul. I want you to know there is a place where God draws the line and tells the devil, "You can come up to the line, but don't cross it." The minute he crosses the line, he has to deal with God. Don't get insomnia or an ulcer because the devil is barking at you. Just remember, he can't cross the line. I don't care how loudly the devil growls or how mean he becomes; the devil can never cross the line. Once God sets the boundary, the devil cannot go any further.

WE ARE BEING KEPT BY THE POWER OF GOD

". . .who are kept by the power of God through faith unto salvation ready to be revealed in the last time" (1 Peter 1:5, KJV). We never have to worry about what's going on because we know there is power keeping us. You can take whatever the devil brings your way because you never have to worry about being strong enough to handle trouble. When you don't have the strength, there is a power keeping you.

You know if it hadn't been for God you would have lost your mind, gone off the deep end, and backslid. You're still alive because you're being kept by the power of God. Do you have any idea how much power that is? Peter said that the God who created the world with His mouth is the God whose power is keeping you.

Some of you are worried because somebody doesn't like you. Why do you care? What can they do to you if you are being kept by the power of God? The things we worry about are an insult to God. It is an insult to God when we sit around crying and whining because limited human beings don't like us. Here's the good news: "Indeed, he who watches over Israel will neither slumber nor sleep" (Psalm 121:4). While you're sleeping and your enemies are plotting, your Keeper is watching. By the time you wake up, your Keeper has already destroyed your enemy's plan. You're not going through anything that could change who you are or what God has for you. You are being kept by His power.

TESTING, TROUBLES, AND TRIALS PRODUCE SOMETHING IN OUR LIVES

Whatever you're going through is only temporary:

> "Wherein you greatly rejoice, though now for a season, if need be, ye are in heaviness through manifold temptations: that the trial of your faith, being much more precious than of gold that perisheth, though it be tried with fire, might be found unto praise and honor and glory at the appearing of Jesus Christ. . ." (1 Peter 1:6-7, KJV)

Trouble doesn't come to last; it is eventually going to work out for your good. Trouble produces something in us that brings praise, glory, and honor to the Lord Jesus Christ. So, what does trouble do in our lives? Why does God allow trouble to come our way?

Trouble secures us

> "But the God of all grace, who hath called us unto His eternal glory by Christ Jesus, after that ye

have suffered a while, make you perfect, stablish, strengthen, settle you." (1 Peter 5:10, KJV)

Peter uses the word *stablish*, which means to firmly fix, to ground, or to make secure. In other words, trouble rivets us into place. Trouble has the capacity to do one of two things: either drive us *to* God, or drive us *from* God. I have watched saints let trouble drive them from God. When trouble comes and you allow it to make you sit down on your praise, you are letting your troubles drive you from God. God never promised that troubles wouldn't come. He never promised that we would never have a struggle. He did promise that He would never leave us, no matter the struggle or how much trouble we face.

If we handle trouble appropriately, it will drive us to God and rivet us into place. It will make us so connected to God that nothing can separate us from Him. When we get stuck to God, the wind can blow and the rain may fall, but nothing comes between the two of us. Some of us have been in a place where trouble came with such fervency and frequency that we latched onto God tightly, until we welded to Him. We couldn't get loose even if we wanted to. The pressure we were under squeezed us right into God. Now we are so imbedded there is nothing that can pull us apart.

Trouble strengthens us

You never know what you can handle until you go through something, and then you discover you can take more than you thought. If you looked back at some of the trouble you have already been through, you would find it hard to believe that you have come out on the other side with your sanity and praise. God took you to unfamiliar places and you discovered that you could handle what you found there. You didn't think you could make it, survive it, or overcome it, but you're on the other side. You made it because trouble didn't come to destroy you; it came to make you stronger.

Some of you are now stronger than ever. The devil should have left you alone. When he applied the pressure, you were driven to your knees. It's like Popeye and spinach. Every time Bluto made him afraid he would say, "I've had all I can stand, and I can't stands no more." Then Popeye would pop that can of spinach, gulp it down, and grow muscles he never knew he had.

Once God sends trouble, it will make you stronger. You have a praying place you've never had before, because trouble taught you how to pray. You have a relationship with God you've never had before, because everybody else walked out and all you had was God. You learned how to lean on Him, because trouble taught you there is a friend who sticks closer than a brother. Trouble strengthens us. It takes our opposition and resistance and builds up our strength and stamina. We're able to take what we never thought we could.

Trouble settles us

Settling is not about God, it's about us. We don't just settle down, we settle in like poured concrete. When you're settled, you can stand, endure, and survive.

That's why Peter says, "After that ye have suffered a while," because only suffering will get you there. You get to a place where you say, "I don't care what happens, I'm not moving." A lot of us aren't there yet, but trouble has a way of settling us and we get to a place where we say, "I don't care what the devil brings, I've made up my mind that I'm staying with God. I'm not going back. I backslid once before and I'm not going back there. I'm going to stand right here. I don't know what tomorrow's going to bring, but when tomorrow comes, it's going to find me standing right here. I'm not going to be a fair-weather saint, who only serves God when things are going well. I'm going to stand my ground.

When the storm is over and they look for me, I'll be right here. I don't care what the devil does. I don't care what other people do. I don't care what the saints or the ain'ts do. When everything is said and done, I'm going to be standing right here. I'm going to be like Job: 'All the days of my appointed time I will wait till my change comes' (Job 14:14, KJV). I don't know when the change is coming, but I know that He knows what it takes; and after He has tried me, I'm coming out like pure gold."

Make up your mind that your soul is going to be anchored in the Lord. Bless the Lord at all times, so that His praise is continually in your mouth. Praise God where you are, because praise will bring power, victory, and deliverance.

PART THREE

—

THE PRICE OF BEING BLESSED

CHAPTER ELEVEN

—

Destiny, Dominion, and Discipline

According to the book *The Burden of Freedom* by Myles Munroe, God brought order to creation before making man. The world was in darkness and the first thing God did was turn on the light so He could see what He was working with; He then brought order out of confusion. Dr. Munroe says, "God organized the rest before He created the best," which means you can never have the best in life until you organize your life. God is not going to bless you with a million dollars if you can't balance your checkbook with fifty dollars. God is not going to just drop you into your blessed place; you need to have a plan to get there.

God put Adam and Eve in a place—Eden; His presence and glory made the spot perfect. All of us have a personal Eden—that place of blessing and blessedness, fulfillment, and purpose. Eden is not always physical or geographical. Our Eden can also be a state of being or a mindset and attitude. Your *locus* really doesn't matter as much as your *focus*. You can get a bigger house, another spouse, another city, or another church; if your attitude is bad, you are the problem. In other words your situation may be bad or negative, but you can still prosper.

There will be places that God turns into Eden while we're on the way to the blessed place, because He blesses us along the way. Christians should want success because we are the light of the world and God's ambassadors. We don't project a very good image of God when we're poor and broke down. John said, "Beloved, I wish above all things that thou mayest prosper and be in health, even as thy soul prospereth" (3 John 2, KJV). God told Joshua, "If you will meditate in the word and live by the word, I will make your way prosperous and you will have good success." That's what you should want: To be prosperous and to have good success, and you can't spell good without God!

John Maxwell says in *The Success Journey* that success is not a destination but a journey. Americans have the mindset that once we get a certain amount of stuff, we have arrived. We need to understand that accumulating things doesn't mean we have arrived. As I'm moving toward my blessed place, I don't just focus on the destination; I allow God to turn every place I go into a blessed place.

God uses every place we go and every period of our lives to bless us so we can inspire and bless someone else. God wants to use us where we are so that others around us (and coming behind us) can benefit from our experience and be blessed by an encounter with us. We often wonder why God has us in a certain place; there is somebody around us that God wants to bless through us.

Adam and Eve were placed in a perfect situation and God issued orders, directions, and instructions on how to maintain the perfection they inherited. For Adam and Eve, it was not a matter of getting to a blessed place; it was a matter of maintaining the blessed place. That's the issue for some of you. It takes effort to maintain everything, including our walk with God. God put Adam and Eve in a perfect spot; yet, they couldn't maintain their place of blessing.

GETTING TO YOUR BLESSED PLACE IS A MATTER OF DESTINY

When I am walking in my destiny, I am at the place where I have the legitimate right to be where I am and to do what I'm doing:

> The word of the LORD came to me, saying, "Before I formed you in the womb I knew you, before you were born I set you apart; I appointed you as a prophet to the nations." "Alas, Sovereign Lord," I said, "I do not know how to speak; I am too young." But the Lord said to me, "Do not say, 'I am too young.' You must go to everyone I send you to and say whatever I command you. Do not be afraid of them, for I am with you and I will rescue you," declares the LORD. (Jeremiah 1:4-8)

God told Jeremiah, "Don't worry about what people think about you or how they act toward you; you are moving toward your destiny. This is why I made you and you have a legitimate right to be where you are and to do what you do." Let me tell you why that's so powerful. Walking in my destiny gives me boldness, confidence, and courage, because I know that God put me where I am. I never have to worry about who is for me or who likes me when I'm walking in destiny; I am where I'm supposed to be. No one can stop me or touch me, because I'm moving in my destiny.

Adam and Eve gave up what was legitimately theirs because they didn't understand their destiny. Some of you have given up dreams, goals, and ambitions, because you didn't understand that the dream people laughed at was your destiny. That idea for a business that people said was the dumbest one they had ever heard of was your ticket out of the ghetto. It was your passport out of poverty, but you let somebody with no plan, no vision, and no idea talk you out of your legitimate right to succeed. Now you're stuck in a dead-end job when you should have a career, because you've given up what was legitimately yours. You should get angry enough to say, "I will not be here this time next year. I'm coming out of this."

GETTING TO THE BLESSED PLACE IS A MATTER OF DOMINION

The Genesis account of creation reveals that God gave Adam and Eve authority, dominion, and rule over all of creation. Yet, they let a serpent talk them out of their blessed place. It's important to understand that Satan needs a form to do anything because he's a spirit, which is why he entered the serpent. The snake wasn't Satan; it was Satan in the snake. Eve listened to a created being that God had already given her authority over. God gave them the right to exercise authority over everything in the garden, whether it was walking, flying, swimming, or crawling. When the serpent started talking, Eve should have said, "You are out of place. You don't dictate to me, I dictate to you."

The devil will use anything and anyone to stop you from moving to your destiny, but you have to remember that you have authority and dominion as a Christian:

> "I will give you the keys of the kingdom of heaven; whatever you bind on earth will be bound in heaven, and whatever you loose on earth will be loosed in heaven." (Matthew 16:19)

We must stop letting people and conditions determine where we go. The Greater One lives inside of us. We have to walk in authority if we are going to get to and stay in our blessed place.

GETTING TO THE BLESSED
PLACE TAKES DISCIPLINE

God didn't create Adam and Eve as robots. They were given free will with the power to choose. The Tree of Knowledge was not in the garden to trip them up; the tree was there to activate Adam's willpower. You can't exercise your will until you have a choice. God put something in the garden that presented a choice for Adam, which activated his will to say, "I *choose* to obey God."

Adam and Eve had to operate in self-control, and we do too. We can't let ourselves do everything we want to do. We have to learn how to say no to ourselves. We will never get to our blessed place without discipline or without learning to use a two-letter, one-syllable word: N-O:

- Look at what you want to do; know it's wrong and say "No."

- Look at what your flesh desires; know that it doesn't please God and say "No."

- Look at what will drain and dry up your resources and squander your anointing and say "No."

- Look at what will hinder and hold you back and say "No."

The "no" releases you to get to your blessed place. Once you can say "no" to yourself, God will trust you with more.

CHAPTER TWELVE

—

Disclosure, Discovery,

and Determination

God's plans for you are much more elaborate than you have ever imagined. You can't let your present situation stop you from believing this; in spite of where you are right now, God still has a plan for your life. I read the following statement in one of my devotional books, "You can never out-dream God. Whatever dream you have for yourself, it's not bigger than God's dream for you." God has big plans for us. The sad reality is that many of us never realize all that God has in store for us.

Let me give you one illustration. For years scientific studies have shown that humans only use fifteen to twenty percent of their brainpower. Intellectually, we live far below our potential. There's more in you than what you have delivered. It would be mind-blowing if we could peek behind the curtain and see what God has for us. For every natural law there is a corresponding spiritual law. So, if mankind never comes close to reaching their natural ability because of sin, choices, indifference, and laziness, then how much more is that true of our spiritual ability? God has already given us the spiritual power to do for ourselves, but we're waiting on someone else to do it for us.

Years ago, Watchman Nee wrote *The Normal Christian Life*. In this book, Nee says that what we call special, unique, and unusual in Church circles should be the norm for every Christian. If you would ever begin to see who you are in God and what He has put in you, then you could lay hands on someone, pray the prayer of faith, and God would heal them. Seeing people get healed, delivered, and saved should happen every day! You don't need a collar, robe, title, or business card to be anointed. You can change the atmosphere simply by walking into a room. As a child of God, people getting saved, healed, and delivered shouldn't surprise us; we should be surprised when it doesn't happen. What we think is great is normal to God. God never intended for there to be spiritual superstars, but the Church has gotten so anemic and lazy that we let other people have the power for us, rather than pay the price to walk in the power that God says we can have:

> "Behold, I give you authority to trample on ser-
> pents and scorpions, and over all the power of the
> enemy, and nothing shall by any means hurt you."
> (Luke 10:19, NKJV)

Many of us never achieve our best for God because we don't understand that God has a place for us called the blessed place. This is not just the place where we get all of the things we want. The blessed place is where you come into the fullness of your own self. It's where you meet, discover, accept, and embrace the real you. It's the place of your purpose and destiny. It's the place where you come to know who you are and then learn to celebrate who you are. Someone once said, "Give me a place where I can stand and I'll move the world." In other words, give me a place where I was meant to be and from there, I can move the world. The blessed place is the full realization of who you are. Because we have put on so many masks and played so many games, we no longer know who we are.

THE BLESSED PLACE IS A PLACE
OF SELF-DISCLOSURE

Knowing who you are is vital. This truth can be seen in the life of Jacob, who arrived at his blessed place unaware that it was his place. Like many of us, Jacob happened upon his place; but how many of you know that nothing just happens?

"The man asked him, 'What is your name?' 'Jacob,' he answered" (Genesis 32:27). That might not seem like a big deal to you, but this was a turning point in Jacob's life. "Jacob" means supplanter, trickster, schemer, denier, conniver, manipulator, and con man; Jacob had more than lived up to his name. When the angel asked Jacob, "What is your name?" God made Jacob's blessed place a place of self-disclosure. Jacob had to confess who he was. He didn't say "My name is Reverend, Bishop, Deacon Jacob." He said, "My name is Jacob," and in that one sentence he gave full-disclosure: I'm tricky, sneaky, conniving, and manipulative.

A large part of getting to your blessed place is admitting who you are and owning up to the good, the bad, and the ugly. That's why William Shakespeare wrote, "To thy own self be true, and it shall follow as night doth day, thou canst be false to any man." You have to know who you are, even if who you are is not very pretty right now:

> Within my earthly temple there's a crowd;
> There's one of us that's humble, one that's proud;
> There's one that's brokenhearted for his sins
> And one who, unrepentant, sits and grins;
> There's one who loves his neighbor as himself
> And one who cares for naught but fame and self.
> From sure corroding care I would be free

If once I could determine which one is me.
(Edward Sanford Martin, 1914, Public domain.)

Do you really know who you are? You'll never get to your blessed place until you have a moment of self-disclosure, and it's not always pretty. All the things Jacob had done to his parents and sibling were revealed in the one sentence, "My name is Jacob."

THE BLESSED PLACE IS A PLACE
OF SELF-DISCOVERY

Then the man said, "Your name will no longer be Jacob, but Israel, because you have struggled with God and with humans and have overcome." (Genesis 32:28)

Jacob had to struggle with the angel to find out who he was and who he was meant to be. His parents named him Jacob, but don't let other people name you. If other people name you, they will define you. If they define you, they will limit you. If they limit you, they will try to control you. Find out who God says you are:

The Lord said to her, "Two nations are in your womb, and two peoples from within you will be separated; one people will be stronger than the other, and the older will serve the younger." (Genesis 25:23)

God told Rebekah before the babies were born that the younger (Jacob) would be greater than the older (Esau) and the older would serve the younger. Everything Jacob did in his life—stealing the birthright, stealing the blessing, lying, conniving—was to get by stealth what was his by God's will.

When you don't know who you are and you let other people

pick your name, you live up to their name instead of God's name. So, God sent the angel to tell him, "I can't take you where I am going to take you with a name like Jacob. I have to change your name. I am going to name you Israel, which means a prince of God, because that is who I determined you to be. I told your mother that it wasn't going to be the traditional way. I told her when you were born I was going to make the younger one greater. You have been trying to do something in your flesh that was already done in the spirit."

You need to relax and trust God. If He said it, He will bring it to pass. Jacob didn't have to scheme and connive. All he had to do was ask his Maker, "What's my name?" Once you know who you are, you will never be the same. When people talk about you, it will roll off your back like water off of a duck. What people say will never stop you, because you're going to discover who you are. You will forget the things that people have said all of your life and you'll tell God, "You are my Creator, my Originator; tell me my name." God will turn the light bulb on and you will discover who you are. And once that happens, the devil is in trouble, because he can't stop you once you know who you are.

THE BLESSED PLACE IS A PLACE
OF SELF-DETERMINATION

"The sun rose above him as he passed Peniel and he was limping because of his hip" (Genesis 32:31). After wrestling with the angel, Jacob discovered that he had been crippled on his way to destiny. However, his wound did not stop him; his hurt did not hinder him; and his pain did not impede him. He crossed Peniel and came at last to Canaan. He didn't look pretty, but he made it. He wasn't strutting, but he made it. He didn't go in walking strong, but he made it. He wrestled with the angel and discovered his identity, and he was determined not to let anything hinder his progress, including his own pain.

We may get tired, weary, discouraged, and hurt; but we can't give up because by the grace of God, we can make it. You may not cross the finish line at full stride, but you'll make it. You may not go across with all of your glory, but you'll make it. You may not go in looking as good as somebody else, but you'll make it. You may not go across with all the strength you used to have, but you'll make it. Even with a limp, you can make it because God is on your side.

Jacob wasted many years doing things his way; all he had to do was ask God for help. His life demonstrates that sometimes our blessed place has more to do with who we are than where we are.

CHAPTER THIRTEEN

—

Failure, Fleeing, and Faith

The Apostle Paul said that we are to learn from the lives of people in the Old Testament to show us both what to do and what not to do. We can gain wisdom for our own lives from their experiences:

> "Now all these things happened to them as examples, and they were written for our admonition, upon whom the ends of the ages have come." (1 Corinthians 10:11, NKJV)

God allowed certain things to be recorded in the Bible, not to fill up pages, but so we could have the benefit of the experiences of those who have gone before us. That's why it's important that we become students of the Word of God, so that we can discover the principles that will govern and guide our lives as we journey from earth to glory.

When I refer to getting to your blessed place, I am not necessarily talking about a place of new clothes, new cars, and more cash. The blessed place is the place of maximized living. It's the place of purpose, destiny, and the will of God; it's the place where you become all that you were meant to be. Sometimes in order for you to get to the blessed place God has to first put you in some unpleasant places. If you have only lived in the lap of luxury, you would need to be strengthened in the furnace of affliction. The difficult places of your life are what really make you stronger—not ease and comfort.

When you get to your blessed place, you will find that money is no problem because your creativity is flowing and your energy is released; nothing becomes impossible. Even when life gives you lemons, you have enough creativity to make lemonade and become a millionaire. You can bloom wherever you are planted. This is why Satan wants to keep you from your blessed place. It's the place where you walk in real freedom and realize who you are:

- <u>God has a purpose, plan, and reason for every life</u>. You were born for a reason because there is something you are meant to do. Your life will become so much brighter when you discover what that is.

- <u>God plans the timing of our birth and our purpose; everything is tied to the time we are needed</u>. He has you alive now because you're needed now. Everybody was born at the right time.

- <u>God does not give up on us even when we give up on ourselves</u>. "For the gifts and calling of God are without repentance" (Romans 11:29, KJV).

When God chose Israel as His people, He didn't ask their permission nor make His choice predicated on their behavior. Even when they rejected His Son, His first plan for them was still His plan. No matter what you do, God will accomplish His purpose because His calling is irrevocable.

If God called you to do something and you have messed up, you need to get up, clean up, and straighten yourself up, because you're still called. Stop wallowing in your mess. Get yourself together. You may feel that God has rescinded His call because you've messed up; but how can a God who knows everything about you before He made you rescind a decision that He has already made? Start doing what God has called you to do.

These truths are shown in the life of Moses in a powerful and dramatic way, and come to a head on the backside of the Midian Desert where Moses meets God in a burning bush. Keep in mind that it's not the location alone that makes this place blessed; it's what happened there.

MOSES FACED HIS FAILURE

Moses was called to be a deliverer, but he went about it the wrong way and failed at his first attempt:

> One day, after Moses had grown up, he went out to where his own people were and watched them at their hard labor. He saw an Egyptian beating a Hebrew, one of his own people. Looking this way and that and seeing no one, he killed the Egyptian and hid him in the sand. The next day he went out and saw two Hebrews fighting. He asked the one in the wrong, "Why are you hitting your fellow Hebrew?" The man said, "Who made you ruler and judge over us? Are you thinking of killing me as you killed the Egyptian?" Then Moses was afraid and thought, "What I did must have become known." When Pharaoh heard of this, he tried to kill Moses, but Moses fled from Pharaoh and went to live in Midian, where he sat down by a well. (Exodus 2:11-15)

There are some of you who have stopped trying because your first attempt at purpose failed. I read a book entitled *Never Wrestle With a Pig*, where the author, Mark H. McCormack, talks about a corner on Lexington Avenue in New York City near his office. He said that over the past ten years five restaurants have opened on this corner. Each restaurant stays open about two years and then closes. It's obvious that there is something about that location that doesn't work, but somebody has to do due diligence to determine if a restaurant could succeed at that location.

You are an entrepreneur and your first business failed, so now you're working for someone else. Maybe you attempted your business too soon. You're blaming your failure on God, but perhaps you didn't do due diligence in getting a sense of what it would take for your business to succeed. Perhaps you started with too little capital and too much overhead. Your failure does not mean God's purpose changed. You must get into God's timing and place, and do it God's way. Some of you know your assignment, but you're trying to do it in the flesh. You failed and now you want to give up, but God has not given up on you.

God gave Moses forty years to wallow in his failure. Then God met him on the backside of the desert while he was leading sheep and said, "You know good and well I didn't make you a shepherd, I made you a deliverer. I didn't put you on earth to lead sheep, but people. I know you think I have changed my mind because you failed, but I have given you forty years to get over the failure. Get up and start doing what I called you to do!"

God has not given up on you. Your assignment still stands even though you failed the first time.

MOSES STOPPED FLEEING

Moses had been running for forty years until God said, "Moses, it's time to stop running." Some of you are running from your assignment, your purpose, and your destiny. You will never reach your blessed place until you stop running. You can be out of the will of God and still do well, but your life is not successful based on how much money you make; your life is successful based on fulfilling your purpose. There is such a thing as being a successful failure:

- You're fleeing because of fear: "I don't know if I can."

- You're fleeing because of your foes: As long as you live, you'll have people against you.

- You're fleeing because of your focus: You're focused on the wrong thing.

If you want to get to your blessed place, you must stop fleeing.

MOSES STEPPED OUT IN FAITH

John Maxwell in *Running With the Giants* writes about Moses letting go of the pain of his past and the comfort of the present to embrace the uncertainty of his future. Moses stepped out in faith because he saw the promise of his purpose:

> Now Moses was tending the flock of Jethro his father-in-law, the priest of Midian, and he led the flock to the far side of the desert and came to Horeb, the mountain of God. There the angel of the Lord appeared to him in flames of fire from within a bush. Moses saw that though the bush was on fire it did not burn up. So Moses thought, "I will go over and see this strange sight—why the bush does not burn up." When the Lord saw that he had gone over to look, God called to him from within the bush, "Moses! Moses!" And Moses said, "Here I am." "Do not come any closer," God

said. "Take off your sandals, for the place where you are standing is holy ground." Then he said, "I am the God of your father, the God of Abraham, the God of Isaac and the God of Jacob." At this, Moses hid his face, because he was afraid to look at God. (Exodus 3:1-6)

Faith is acting on what you believe. A chair is always going to be a chair; however, faith in action is sitting down, allowing the chair to take the full weight of your body, and believing that the chair will hold you up.

Some of you say that you believe in God, but you've never stepped out in faith and took God at His Word. If you believe in God, get your business plan together and take it to the bank. If you believe in God, get your resume together and find a better job. If you believe in God, step out in faith by paying your tithes and taking God at His Word. If you believe in God, stop talking about it and put feet to your faith and turn your faith into action.

Somewhere out there is your purpose and why you were born. You have to let go of what you have in order to get what God has for you. God has miracles for you, but you can't get them until you step out in faith:

- God had a Red Sea parting, but Moses had to leave Midian.

- God had manna from heaven, but Moses had to leave Midian.

- God had water coming out of a rock, but Moses had to leave Midian.

- God had a pillar of fire and clouds to lead him, but Moses had to leave Midian.

- God had Pharaoh and the Egyptians drowning in the Red Sea, but Moses had to leave Midian.

God has something for you, too—miracles, promotions, scholarships, jobs, opportunities, mates, houses, and land—but you have to step out in faith. You may not see it, but if God said it, you can claim it and shout like it's already yours!

CHAPTER FOURTEEN

—

Dreams, Delays, and Disappointments

Joseph is a powerful model of integrity. His life was not perfect or easy. His struggles made him stand out. He was misunderstood by his father, rejected by his brothers, lied on by his employer, and forgotten by his friends. His life seemed to go from bad to worse. Yet, not once do we see bitterness, anger, or vindictiveness. Despite everything Joseph went through he was able to keep a gentle and loving spirit. He sounds almost too good to be true; but let me remind you that while Joseph is a type of Jesus, he was still human. He got frustrated and fed up, but Joseph had the special ingredient we must all possess if we're going to get to our blessed place: An absolute trust in the faithfulness of God.

It doesn't matter what's going on in your life; if you know how to trust God when the storm is raging, God can give you peace in the midst of the storm. Some of you feel that the only way God shows you His love is by taking you out of or around the storm. But I submit that when God really wants to shape, make, and mold us, He puts us in the middle of a storm and says, "If you trust me, I may not stop or calm the storm; but I will give you peace in the midst of the storm so that you can praise me no matter what is going on around you." Real praise doesn't come from the safe places of life; anybody can praise God when everything is going your way. But when the bottom drops out and the roof caves in, can you still praise God? When you have trust in God, your circumstances don't change your attitude. If you really trust God, then you trust Him on the mountain or in the valley. Where you are doesn't stop your trust because it's not predicated on your position or condition. Your trust is based on your relationship. No matter what Joseph went through, he knew how to trust God.

When I looked at Joseph's life through the lens of new inspiration, I discovered that his life can be broken down into three distinct sections. Each represents a phase on the journey that leads to the blessed place. I discovered that you don't wake up in the morning and arrive at your blessed place by noon. God is not interested in getting you someplace overnight; He wants to develop character in you so that you can handle whatever life brings your way.

DREAMS, DESTINY, AND DETERMINATION

Joseph is one of the few Bible personalities that we are allowed to follow from birth to death. We are also allowed to meet his family. Sometimes family can be your worst enemy on the road to the blessed place, because they know you so well. They base their assessment of you on your past performance. And because of what they know about your past, they think they know your potential. But you can't let what your family knows about your yesterday determine your today, or your tomorrow.

Parents owe their children encouragement to dream, and to pursue their dreams. Most of us grew up without being released to dream. When I told my mother and grandmother that I was going to be a preacher, they didn't laugh and tell me to go sit down since there weren't any preachers in our family. My Aunt Betty went over to the church and brought back my grandfather's black choir robe. Aunt Betty said that my grandmother had told her I had been playing "church" and she decided that every preacher needed a robe. From the basement of my grandmother's house, I would "preach" to my "church," which consisted of my sisters. When they weren't there, I would preach to empty chairs or to my sisters' dolls. I even ran an outdoor crusade and preached to the hedges and flowers! I'm thankful for having people in my life who encouraged my dreams. Today, as I preach all over the world, I remember that my family encouraged me and said, "If you can dream it, God can bring it to pass!" We must learn how to encourage our children in their dreams. Dreams demand determination. Dreams are nice, but you have to wake up and go to work. Dreaming about a house is wonderful, but you have to save money for a down payment. Dreaming about owning your own business is nice, but you have to learn how to balance a checkbook.

Dreams came to Joseph as a child and they provided a glimpse into his destiny. You can't give up at the first sign of struggle:

> Joseph had a dream, and when he told it to his brothers, they hated him all the more. He said to them, "Listen to this dream I had: We were binding sheaves of grain out in the field when suddenly my sheaf rose and stood upright, while your sheaves gathered around mine and bowed down to it." His brothers said to him, "Do you intend to reign over us? Will you actually rule us?" And they hated him all the more because of his dream and what he had said. (Genesis 37:5-8)

When people try to hinder the dream inside you, don't surrender to the meanness and smallness of other people. If they laugh at your first dream, dream another dream:

> Then he had another dream, and he told it to his brothers. "Listen," he said, "I had another dream, and this time the sun and moon and eleven stars

were bowing down to me." When he told his father as well as his brothers, his father rebuked him and said, "What is this dream you had? Will your mother and I and your brothers actually come and bow down to the ground before you?" His brothers were jealous of him, but his father kept the matter in mind. (Genesis 37:9-11)

How many of you have put your life on hold because one person laughed at your dream? Don't give anyone that much power. Dreams reveal your destiny, but reaching that destiny demands determination. The first phase of Joseph's life was made up of dreams that revealed his destiny and filled him with determination.

God has given you a dream. Your dream is a glimpse into your destiny, but you won't get there by osmosis. You have to work and that takes determination.

DELAYS, DISAPPOINTMENTS, DETOURS, AND DIVINE DIRECTION

It would be nice if Joseph's story read, "He had a dream and it came to pass." Very few of us will get to our blessed place without going through a struggle. Approximately fifteen years passed between Joseph's dreams and reality. The waiting period was filled with delays, disappointments, detours, and divine direction.

Joseph dreamed, received a glimpse into his destiny, and was filled with determination. Along the way to fulfillment there was the pit, Potiphar, and prison, prior to Pharaoh. At the end of the journey, he was able to look over his life and say to his brothers, "You intended to harm me, but God intended it for good to accomplish what is now being done, the saving of many lives" (Genesis 50:20).

Does your life seem to be in chaos right now, with nothing going right or making sense? Cheer up. God is still in control and He is taking you somewhere.

Life is filled with delays, disappointments, detours, and divine direction. It was God who sent you everywhere you have been. As you look back over your life, you can see the hand of God bringing you to where you are now. He has brought you to where you are for a purpose and a reason.

PURPOSE, PROMOTION, AND PROSPERITY

If you stop reading Joseph's story before the end, you will miss something powerful. Prior to the end of the story it looks like Joseph is a failure, a fool, and a fake because nothing he dreamed came true. . .until Pharaoh had a dream:

> Then it came to pass, at the end of two full years, that Pharaoh had a dream; and behold, he stood by the river. Suddenly there came up out of the river seven cows, fine looking and fat; and they fed in the meadow. Then behold, seven other cows came up after them out of the river, ugly and gaunt, and stood by the other cows on the bank of the river. And the ugly and gaunt cows ate up the seven fine looking and fat cows. So Pharaoh awoke.

> He slept and dreamed a second time; and suddenly seven heads of grain came up on one stalk, plump and good. Then behold, seven thin heads, blighted by the east wind, sprang up after them. And the seven thin heads devoured the seven plump and full heads. So Pharaoh awoke, and indeed, it was a dream.

> Now it came to pass in the morning that his spirit was troubled, and he sent and called for all the magicians of Egypt and all its wise men. And Pharaoh

told them his dreams, but there was no one who could interpret them for Pharaoh. Then the chief butler spoke to Pharaoh, saying: "I remember my faults this day. When Pharaoh was angry with his servants, and put me in custody in the house of the captain of the guard, both me and the chief baker, we each had a dream in one night, he and I. Each of us dreamed according to the interpretation of his own dream. Now there was a young Hebrew man with us there, a servant of the captain of the guard. And we told him, and he interpreted our dreams for us; to each man he interpreted according to his own dream. And it came to pass, just as he interpreted for us, so it happened. He restored me to my office, and he hanged him."

Then Pharaoh sent and called Joseph, and they brought him quickly out of the dungeon; and he shaved, changed his clothing, and came to Pharaoh. And Pharaoh said to Joseph, "I have had a dream, and there is no one who can interpret it. But I have heard it said of you that you can understand a dream, to interpret it." So Joseph answered Pharaoh, saying, "It is not in me; God will give Pharaoh an answer of peace." (Genesis 41:1-16, NKJV)

Joseph's interpretation of Pharaoh's dream became the opportunity for Joseph to move into his purpose. Getting to his purpose led to promotion, and promotion produced prosperity.

Your dream is your ticket off of welfare. Your dream is your ticket out of an apartment. Your dream is your ticket out of that low-level, low-paying job. Your dream is your ticket out of the dark hole that life has sucked you into. Your dream is your ticket out.

Pharaoh had a dream, which became an occasion for Joseph's purpose to come to pass. Everything that happened in his life was for this purpose: To place him in position to interpret Pharaoh's dream. You're wondering why you are still where you are. Perhaps it's the place of your purpose. Someone may run into a problem they can't handle and they will look to you, which will be the occasion for your purpose to be manifested, which will lead to your promotion, which will lead to your prosperity.

In one hour Joseph moved from prisoner to Prime Minister. He was promoted from a jail cell to a chariot in one hour. From a prison suit to a custom-tailored suit in one hour. From a nobody to a somebody in one hour. From poverty to prosperity in one hour. From infamy to fame in one hour. From being at the bottom to being on the top in one hour.

It has taken a long time to get to where you are, but it won't take God long to get you to where you have to go. I know you've been waiting a long time, but just give God one hour. He doesn't need all day, month, or year; God only needs one hour. What He can do in one hour will blow your mind.

PART FOUR

—

TURNING WHERE YOU ARE INTO THE BLESSED PLACE

CHAPTER FIFTEEN

—

Bethlehem of Judea:
The Place of Beginning

Jesus teaches us that who you are matters much more than where you are. It's more important to know who you are and to be able to handle the situation you're in, no matter where you are. In the wilderness or on a cross, Jesus knew how to turn every place into the blessed place.

The first place that becomes a blessed place in Jesus' life is the place of His birth: A stable in a little town called Bethlehem. Keep in mind who He is and what He has come to do. For the rest of His life He has to deal with the place of His birth and the circumstances surrounding it; and as quiet as it's kept, so do we. The first place everyone must make into a blessed place is the place of our birth. You can't get past it, but a lot of us are uncomfortable with the surroundings of our birth. We have to get comfortable with the circumstances of our birth before God will take us the rest of the way

As we look back on Jesus' birth, it becomes easy for us to romanticize the events surrounding His birth; yet, for those who experienced it—Mary and Joseph—it was anything but glamorous. In reality it was a dark, painful experience.

Put yourself in their shoes. For Mary, the trip was a nightmare in and of itself. She was pregnant, uncomfortable, and away from family and home. Then her water breaks and she has to deliver the baby somewhere; but everywhere they turn, there's no room for them. What about Joseph, the man of the house? He has a new wife expecting a baby and he is unable to provide a place for his wife to give birth. This man must suffer the indignation of watching his wife give birth in a stable. I'm sure the only thing that made the entire experience bearable was the knowledge of who this child was and how important His birth would be to the world.

It occurs to me that the "something" that kept Joseph and Mary during this difficult time is the "something" that kept my forebearers and allowed them to bring children into a world in the midst of slavery and oppression. My ancestors were able to marry and produce children knowing they would be coming into a world filled with slavery, oppression, injustice, and inequity. Yet, their faith allowed them to believe that every child was a child of promise; and if a child could come into the world, that child would make a difference. It doesn't matter who you are or where you come from. If God allows you to be born, then you are born for a reason and a purpose. It doesn't matter how bad the world is; your existence makes a difference. All you have to do is realize who you are and understand that God made you for a reason and a purpose.

Every race has gone through their own dark night of the soul; yet, they all continued having children because they believed that one child could make a difference in the world.

Aren't you glad that Mary didn't abort Jesus? Aren't you glad that in spite of the inconvenience and obstacles, she pressed through and brought forth that baby? What a difference that baby has made to this world!

You're not the Son of God, but you are somebody and your life counts. Your mother went through the pain of giving birth; you need to make up your mind to live your life to the glory of God and to fulfill His purpose in your life. All of us are a part of this world for a reason and a purpose.

THE PLACE OF OUR BIRTH IS THE PLACE OF OUR BEGINNINGS

We have no control over the place of our birth. We're just born—when, where, and to whom—without any input from us. If God had given us the option, a lot of us would have picked other parents. Don't feel bad about that, because if parents were given the option they would have picked other babies! That's what is so interesting about this story; Jesus doesn't get to choose the place of His birth. The decision of whether to be born in a palace or a manger was taken out of His hands, because God chose His birthplace.

While you're wrestling with the place of your beginning, remember that the when, where, and to whom was not based on the luck of the draw or the roll of the dice. It happened by the predetermined will of God. In order for us to be who we are, we had to be born where we were born, to whom we were born, and when we were born—all because of God's plan. We need to be at peace with our birthplace because it is the place of our beginning

God chose the place for Jesus' birth and did the same thing for us. Jesus could have been born in Rome or Greece, but every now and then, God allows us to be born in unlikely places. He then takes us from where we are born to places we've never dreamed we could go. Where you start is not as important as where you finish. All of it is part of God's plan. If you had not been born where you were, with the beginning you had, chances are you would not be the man or woman you are today.

I recently had the privilege of going back home to New York to spend time with my entire family. I walked around and rode through the streets of New York and realized that we had some lean, hard, and tough days in the beginning. For years I was insecure about my beginning until I realized that it took my beginning to make me what and who I am. I am the way I am, I think the way I think, and I feel the way I feel because I know where I came from and how far God has brought me. If I hadn't started where I did, I wouldn't be where I am today.

THE PLACE OF OUR BIRTH IS THE PLACE OF OUR BACKGROUND

Your birth story is more than who you are; it includes what you went through to get here. We are a modern day Jabez, because some of us had pain in our delivery. Pain, abuse, rejection, neglect, poverty, sickness, and broken homes are all part of the background story for many of us. Like Jabez (whose name means pain), we discovered we could call on the name of the Lord and say, "Oh, that you would bless me indeed."

Bethlehem of Judea was the place of Jesus' birth and background. William Augustus Jones calls Jesus "back door divinity," meaning that when the world would not let Him in through the front door, He came in through the back. We should be happy about that, because we have a Savior who opens up the back door for us.

THE PLACE OF OUR BIRTH IS THE PLACE OF OUR BAGGAGE

Some people can't handle their beginning or background; they're always playing the victim and placing blame on other people. They never let go of the pain of their past. They can't handle their upbringing. They can't handle that they didn't have a lot of money or their parents never hugged them or bounced them on their knees. I know that hurts; we all need a hug, but stop using that as your excuse for neurosis and pathological behavior. Can you handle your beginnings? Can you handle people calling you names, talking about your hand-me-down clothes and run-over shoes? If you're going to get to the blessed place, you have to learn how to let things go.

Jesus could have let His birthplace become a hindrance. He could have spent His life on a psychiatrist's couch. He could have said, "The pain started on a dark night in a little town called Bethlehem when my parents couldn't find a hotel and I was born in a stable between the horses and the cows." Does your story get worse than that? You may have been born in a public hospital, but at least it was a hospital. You may have had a midwife instead of a nurse, but you still had somebody. I'm not minimizing your pain; I'm maximizing what you have so you can stop dwelling on what you don't have. I'm trying to get you to count your blessings instead of counting your problems.

Jesus was born in a manger in a stable between the horses and the cows, with the smell and stench of animals all around Him. He could have let it stop Him, but Jesus knew it was just the place of His beginning, birth, and background. It was not going to become the place of His baggage because He couldn't let it or anything stop Him from what He had to do. He had a date with destiny.

Jesus turned His birthplace into a blessed place. You can do the same thing. Accept where you were born. Embrace where you were born. Celebrate where you were born, because the place of your birth is not important; the fact that you were born is.

CHAPTER SIXTEEN

—

Egypt: The Place of Transition

As God in the flesh, Jesus experienced everything we go through. He encountered all the things that have happened to us, which allows Him to identify with us and intercede for us.

The fact that Jesus is God in the flesh means we don't serve a God who is indifferent to what we're going through. We serve a God who is able to identify with our struggles, pain, and problems. As humans, we're all vulnerable to the attacks of life. No one will get through life without challenges, struggles, and problems; but as we go through, we are not alone. Jesus not only identifies with us, but He is able to help us. This is where Jesus differs from everyone else. People can identify with us, but they aren't always able to help us. There is a God who not only understands where we are, but He is able to help us while we go through the struggle. Some people want to pretend they can handle life by themselves; but some of us don't mind confessing that we can't handle what life brings our way without Jesus. He is able to be strong in our weaknesses; He is our strength in the terrible places; and He helps us stand when we feel like giving up. He is able to identify with us and intercede for us:

"He is despised and rejected by men; a man of sorrows and acquainted with grief." (Isaiah 53:3 (a), NKJV)

Jesus is able to identify with us when we're sick and suffering, and in our sin:

"For we do not have a High Priest who cannot sympathize with our weaknesses, but was in all points tempted as we are, yet without sin." (Hebrews 4:15, NKJV)

If Jesus had not become sin, then we would not be saved:

"For He made Him who knew no sin to be sin for us, that we might become the righteousness of God in Him." (2 Corinthians 5:21, NKJV)

When we fail, we have a God who understands and is able to help us and give us another chance.

Jesus is our example, especially when it comes to turning the painful places in our lives into the blessed place. Jesus shows us how we can do the same thing. Jesus shows us that it doesn't matter where you start, but where you finish. Some people get stuck where they start and never move to where God is trying to take them. They sit around regurgitating the painful places of their pilgrimage and crying in their milk, singing another sad song while staying stuck in the past. God has an entire world out there to be enjoyed, but you must make up your mind to change. The place of your birth may have been dark, but at least you survived. If God kept you alive, He had a good reason. You have more living to do. Don't die in your past; move to the life God has for you. Get out of the past!

The second place that became a blessed place for Jesus is a

place of transition. Egypt could have been a stopping place if Jesus' parents hadn't understood the difference between a stopping place and a staying place. A lot of us have reached a place in our lives where we had to stop, and we think it is where we are supposed to stay. Often we'll go to a place that is intended as a temporary stopover, but we've somehow made it permanent. Every place we stop is not where we are to stay. Some of us have not reached our purpose, potential, or promise because we stayed at a place where we were only supposed to stop.

God told the angel to tell Joseph to take Mary and Jesus to a place—not to stay, but to stop. When Jesus was born, Magi came to worship Him. When Herod heard of the new king in town he told the wise men to bring him word so he could go worship Jesus, too. Herod wanted to kill Jesus, but God had other plans. The angel told Joseph to take his family to Egypt and stay there until he received word to return. Egypt is in Africa, which means that Joseph and his family are moving further and further away from home, with God guiding and directing every step.

Each of us has an Egypt in our lives; it is the place where God sends us. When He sends us, we may resent or resist it, but we'll discover we are there for our own good. We can't get what God has for us without going to Egypt.

EGYPT IS THE PLACE OF GOD'S PROTECTION

God looks out for us in Egypt so our enemies can't kill us before our time. Egypt is the place God has prepared for us:

> So he got up, took the child and his mother during the night and left for Egypt, where he stayed until the death of Herod. And so was fulfilled what the Lord had said through the prophet: "Out of Egypt I called my son." (Matthew 2:14-15)

Sometimes God removes us from people and places that are no good for us as a way of protecting us. If God moved you to another city and you've been crying about it, stop. God moved you because there were assassins at home whose sole purpose was to kill you. God took you from your hometown to a strange town to protect you, because of what He has put inside of you. Sometimes He will even remove you from your own family. You know why? Protection. God has put something in you, and He can't and won't allow your enemies to get to you too early.

The worst fight you'll have is with the person whose place you're going to take. They see what you don't see yet. You see yourself as a baby, but they see you grown up. They see your potential and the possibilities. You don't recognize who you are, but they know that when you grow up, you'll take their place. You need to understand that if God put you there, they can't keep you out of your place. It's really not their place anyway; they're just holding it for you.

You may be getting further from Nazareth, but Egypt is a necessary stop along the way. God protects and covers us in Egypt and blocks the things that would have destroyed us.

While Jesus was a baby, God had to protect Him. Thirty-three years later there would be another Herod, but this time God doesn't send Jesus to Egypt because now He can handle Herod. That's why you don't stay in Egypt, because to stay there is to stay a baby. There comes a time when you grow up and face your Herod.

EGYPT IS THE PLACE OF GOD'S PROVISION

Egypt is the place where God provides for us. Had Jesus gone anywhere else other than Egypt, the provision and protection wouldn't have been there. There is a place where God says He will bless you:

> Then the Lord said to Elijah, "Go to the east and hide by Kerith Brook, near where it enters the Jordan River. Drink from the brook and eat what the ravens bring you, for I have commanded them to bring you food." So Elijah did as the Lord told him and camped beside Kerith Brook, east of the Jordan. The ravens brought him bread and meat each morning and evening, and he drank from the brook. But after a while the brook dried up, for there was no rainfall anywhere in the land. Then the Lord said to Elijah, "Go and live in the village of Zarephath, near the city of Sidon. I have instructed a widow there to feed you." (1 Kings 17:2-9, NLT)

A lot of Christians are in the wrong place. They want to stay where God *was* instead of where God *is*. Stop getting stuck where you used to get blessed and find out where God is blessing now. That's where you need to go. God provides for you ahead of time because He knows you'll need it. Everybody needs an Egypt, a place you can just run into.

When Joseph, Mary, and Jesus arrived in Egypt, everything they needed was already there. If God has led you to an Egypt will you trust Him to provide for you there, no matter how uncomfortable or unfamiliar it is? I know you're scared and uncertain, but Egypt is where God will bless you. If you stay with God's direction, He will provide for you.

EGYPT IS THE PLACE OF GOD'S PREPARATION

By the time He was ten, Jesus had traveled more than the average person of His day. Egypt was a different culture, race, and people. Yet, God sent Him there to prepare Him for His next assignment: To be the Universal Savior. Because God knows where He is taking us, He knows what it will take for us to do what He has for us to do.

Jesus was born a Jew, but He wasn't just sent to save Jews. Early in His life He lived in another culture. During His most impressionable years, bigotry was removed from His life. He learned that people are only different by color and not by heart; it's not the color of a person's skin that is important, but the content of their character. Sometimes God will put you in a place that you didn't plan on, because God knows what He is going to ask you to do. He wants you to be able to handle your next assignment. He knows you won't get prepared by staying at home among your own kind, so He will send you to other places to broaden your horizon, so you'll see a different world.

Somebody once asked me how I started hanging around preachers from other denominations and this is what I told him. When I was a little boy I grew up around James E. Cray, a pastor who had an ecumenical spirit. Dad Cray enjoyed good preaching and took me to hear Sandy Ray, Gardner Taylor, William Jones, F. D. Washington, Reuben Speaks, O. M. Kelley, and other mighty men of faith. Dad Cray belonged to the interfaith council of the five boroughs of New York and had Catholic priests and Jewish rabbis in and out of our church and his house, because he understood that out of one blood God made everybody.

God knew what He was going to ask me to do, so He put me in an environment that wasn't narrow and confined, but opened my eyes to a world bigger than my own fellowship. I understood early on that the Church is not a denomination but is made up of every blood-washed child of God, no matter who they are. If you are saved, you are in the Church. God opened my eyes because He knew He would give me a platform that was so large that I couldn't be narrow-minded, bigoted, nasty, and critical. I was to love everybody because God loves everybody; it's not His will that any should perish, but that all should come to repentance.

God will take you to places that you don't understand, but

it's all part of your preparation. I didn't know why I had to go through what I went through, but as I look back on my life, I see He was preparing me to do what I'm doing now. I didn't like going through the pain, but I can look back now and see that it was part of the preparation.

When your husband walked out on you and left you to raise the children by yourself, you thought God was being unfair and unkind; but it was part of the preparation so you could someday encourage another young mother by saying, "Daughter, the Lord will provide."

When you suffered through sickness, you thought God was picking on you; but you realize now it was part of the preparation. You walked through the valley of the shadow of death and looked death in the face; and God brought you back from the brink of death so you could tell somebody that He is able to heal all manner of diseases.

You lost your job and had to go on public assistance; you thought it was unfair, but God was preparing you to tell somebody else that He is a Waymaker and a Provider.

You thought you were being picked *on* by God, but now you realize that you were being picked *out*. God has plans for you, and He will take you someplace you have never been. But you first have to go to Egypt.

CHAPTER SEVENTEEN

—

Nazareth:
The Place of Purpose and Fulfillment

From reading the story of Jesus' early life recorded in Matthew, I think it's obvious that landing in Nazareth was not the first choice of Joseph and Mary. The Bible says that an angel appeared and told them it was safe to return to Israel because those who sought to kill the child were dead. We can rejoice that people who trouble us will not be around forever:

> Do not fret because of evil men or be envious of
> those who do wrong; for like the grass they will
> soon wither, like green plants, they will soon die
> away. (Psalm 37:1-2)

The angel told Joseph and Mary it was safe to go back to Israel. They wanted to go to Judea, but it was ruled by one of Herod's sons, who also wanted to kill Jesus. Joseph was afraid to go to Judea so they went to the region of Galilee, a state in the nation. After moving around the state, they finally settled in the city of Nazareth (Matthew 2:19-23). I am not trying to give you a geography lesson, but I am trying to build up your faith. Sometimes you get to the right state, in the right nation, but then you must find the right city. When it looks like you're just wandering and roaming, it's all part of God's plan, because He knows exactly where He is taking you.

Jesus went to Nazareth—the third place He turns into the blessed place. He lived there for the better part of His life. Nazareth was a small, obscure town in the region of Galilee. Not much good had ever come out of Nazareth. But God seems to favor using unlikely places, much like He seems to favor using unlikely people to accomplish His purpose. God seems to have this bend in His nature that makes Him bypass the people you or I think He will pick, in favor of people that nobody would have imagined.

Jesus was taken to Nazareth where He would live, grow, and develop. And Jesus would come onto the public stage out of Nazareth. For the rest of His life He would forever be known as Jesus of Nazareth. Before He was Jesus the Christ, before He was Lord and Master, and before He was Teacher and Rabbi, He was the carpenter from Nazareth. How we handle humility will determine how much honor we are given. God seldom chooses those who are already great. God takes us from where we are and He makes us great.

Some people will never get beyond their past. This is why Nazareth is so painful. When Nathaniel was told by Philip that he had found the Messiah, Nathaniel replied, "Can anything good come out of Nazareth?" (John 1:46, NKJV). There are some people who will always judge us based on where we came from, what school we went to, and what fraternity or sorority we belong to. They want to pigeonhole us, but they don't have the right.

Your worst opposition will come from people who knew you when. There are some people who can't handle your success. As long as you're on welfare, they're happy; as long as you're having babies out of wedlock, they're happy; as long as you're dropping out of school, they're happy; as long as you're on drugs, they're happy, because everybody in Nazareth drops out of school, gets pregnant out of wedlock, is on welfare, and is on drugs. The minute you decide to break the mold, they can't handle your success because they don't believe you deserve it. They can't see themselves having what you have; and if they can't see themselves having it, they can't see you having it either. You cannot let people limit you. Some people are stuck where they are and they need to get unstuck. Some of the worst attacks we get are from our own.

So, how do we turn Nazareth into a blessed place? By remembering what our Nazareth represents.

NAZARETH REPRESENTS A PLACE OF LOVING

We don't know how old Jesus was when He moved to Nazareth, but we know that He spent a good portion of His life there, especially His formative years. In Nazareth He was loved by His family, but also learned how to love in return. Nazareth taught Jesus how to love the world, His family and plain, ordinary, average people. If Jesus had grown up among the elite and sophisticated, He wouldn't have learned how to love average people. God kept closing doors until Joseph and Mary arrived in Nazareth; God had people there that Jesus needed to learn how to love.

Every now and then God takes us through something to increase our capacity to care for others who may one day go through the same thing. That's why we can't resist the thing God takes us through, because it may be our place of preparation. If we have never failed, we cannot have sympathy for those who are failing. If we have never messed up, we cannot have mercy on those who mess up. If we have never been to the bottom, we cannot help someone who has reached the bottom. Once we have been there and made it through by the grace of God, we then can reach back for someone else.

NAZARETH REPRESENTS A PLACE OF LEARNING

We know that Joseph was a carpenter and that in the Jewish tradition, he taught Jesus the trade. We know that Jesus went to synagogue school in Nazareth, so He studied Hebraic history, the Scriptures, and languages. In Nazareth Jesus learned about life—sharing, helping, and obeying. He also learned about loss, because Joseph died in Nazareth. Isn't it ironic that sometimes our most powerful lessons are learned in the places of our greatest pain? Sometimes God teaches us through the pain.

Whatever represents our Nazareth is painful, but didn't you learn something there that you couldn't learn anywhere else? I know your divorce was painful, but didn't you learn to forgive in the Nazareth of your divorce? I know betrayal was painful, but didn't betrayal teach you that you need to really put your trust in God, not people? I know failure was painful, but didn't you learn something about the grace and mercy of God in failure that you couldn't learn in success? I know your sin was painful, but didn't you learn something about forgiveness in your sin that you couldn't learn in self-righteousness?

Sometimes our greatest lessons are learned in our painful places. When we fell down, we learned how to get back up. When we got hurt, we learned how to play with pain. When everybody counted us out, we found strength on the inside to keep on fighting.

NAZARETH REPRESENTS A PLACE OF LEAVING

Nazareth must always be left behind, and it's always painful, because it means letting go of the familiar and the comfortable. It also means stepping into your destiny. You can't step in unless you leave.

I grew up in Far Rockaway, New York. My life revolved around my grandmother's house, the church I grew up in, my spiritual father's house, and my friends' houses. I was happy there because I had a place. But there came a day when I had to leave Far Rockaway, because destiny was calling me to a place called Warren, Ohio, to pastor my first church. Just as I began to settle in Warren, God moved me to Columbus. I had to leave people I had been with for four years to move further into my destiny. If I had never left Far Rockaway, New York or Warren, Ohio, I would have missed my destiny in Columbus, Ohio.

You have been stuck in Nazareth long enough and God has something else for you. It might be unfamiliar and uncomfortable, but you can't be afraid of the future or your destiny. You must have enough faith and courage to claim what God has for you. Someone has said that the promises of God will never take you where the grace of God cannot keep you. He won't fail you. He will open up doors and make a way out of no way.

Some of you will never fulfill your purpose where you are, so the best thing you can do is prepare to leave. Did I want to leave Far Rockaway? No. I could have stayed with my spiritual father and been his assistant, and I would have been happy; but God had something for me infinitely more fulfilling. God moved me to the platform to do what I'm doing now, but only after I was willing to leave my Nazareth. If I hadn't learned how to serve my spiritual father and honor him, I would not be where I am today. Humility always comes before honor.

Some of you are in Nazareth and you've experienced the loving and learning; now it's time to leave. Nazareth is where God prepares you, but it isn't where He uses you.

CHAPTER EIGHTEEN

—

Jordan: The Place of Affirmation

The blessed place is not necessarily a place, location, or destination, as much as it is an attitude and disposition that allows us to turn the worst spot into the blessed place. With the right attitude and disposition, you can make wherever you are the blessed place. That is what Mother Theresa did when she brought beauty and love into the slums of Calcutta. If we can learn that lesson, then we can go to our homes, work, or classrooms, and still sing, shout, and smile, because we have learned how to bring a little bit of heaven into a difficult situation.

The Jordan River becomes the fourth place Jesus turns into the blessed place and we can learn several lessons from Him. "Then cometh Jesus from Galilee to Jordan unto John, to be baptized of him" (Matthew 3:13, KJV). John initially refused to baptize Jesus because he recognized who Jesus was and he didn't feel worthy of baptizing Him. But notice Jesus' reply: "Suffer it to be so now: for thus it becometh us to fulfill all righteousness" (Matthew 3:15, KJV).

Jesus knew who He was

There is no false humility in Jesus. When John first refused to baptize Jesus, He didn't say, "Oh, John I'm not really anybody special, just go ahead and baptize me and get it over with." Jesus said, "I understand why you are reluctant to baptize me, but in order for me to do what I am supposed to do, we must do this. I know who I am."

One of the problems with the Church is that most of us don't know who we are, because we have not learned how to accurately assess ourselves. Most of us—especially those of us who were raised in holiness churches—grew up believing that in order for us to be really saved, we had to deny who we were; and the only way to bring glory to God was by belittling ourselves. When we do that, we are not bringing glory to God but leveling charges against Him, since the Bible says we are made in His image and after His likeness. So, if I say I am nobody, that means I came from nobody, since everything produces after its own kind. We don't know how to accurately assess ourselves.

Jesus knew what He had to do

Jesus left Nazareth when He was thirty years old because He had a purpose that couldn't be fulfilled in Nazareth. His next stop was the Jordan River. Jesus knew that His destiny wasn't in Nazareth; He had to be born in Bethlehem, live in Egypt, grow up in Nazareth, and be baptized in the Jordan River. Do you have any idea what you are supposed to be doing?

Jesus didn't let who He was get in the way of what He had to do

Sometimes we let our identity, our past, and our pride stand in the way of what we need to do. Jesus knew He was the Son of God, but He also knew He needed to be baptized by John in the Jordan River. We need people in our lives who may look like they have nothing to give us, but who are key to unlocking the door that will lead us to our next level of destiny.

Sometimes we hinder our own progress and we get in the way. Jesus went to the Jordan and had an experience there that turned the Jordan River into a blessed place.

ACKNOWLEDGEMENT

Up to this point, Jesus has been the son of Mary and Joseph; but now He is revealed for who He really is: The Son of God.

> As soon as Jesus was baptized, he went up out of the water. At that moment heaven was opened, and he saw the spirit of God descending like a dove and alighting on him. And a voice from heaven said, "This is my Son, whom I love; with him I am well pleased." (Matthew 3:16-17, NIV)

His obedience and willingness to submit caused God to acknowledge Him. Notice that prior to this point God has never said a word about Jesus.

> And when they saw him, they were amazed: and his mother said unto him, Son, why hast thou thus dealt with us? behold, thy father and I have sought thee sorrowing. And he said unto them, How is it that ye sought me? wist ye not that I must be about my Father's business? (Luke 2:48-49, KJV)

God didn't co-sign his statement; heaven didn't open and confirm what Jesus had said:

> And he went down with them, and came to Nazareth, and was subject unto them: but

his mother kept all these sayings in her heart.
(Luke 2:51, KJV)

At no point did God tell Mary she was wrong for correcting Jesus because this was not the time for Jesus to be revealed. I believe Jesus made a premature announcement at the age of twelve because He still had more to learn. God didn't reveal who Jesus was at twelve. God said His first public statement about Jesus when He was thirty years old, immediately after He had obeyed and submitted to baptism. God then said, "Let me introduce you: This is my Beloved Son. Up to now you thought He was just Mary and Joseph's son, but He is so much more." There was no way people could have surmised that there was something special about Jesus, because at no point did He exert power before it was time. Jesus was as much God in the manger as He was walking on water; He was as much God at twelve as He was at thirty, but all of His life He harnessed His power and kept it under wraps until the Father gave Him permission to reveal it.

That kind of restraint is what we haven't learned. Some of you are premature with your announcements. You want us to think you are so much and to recognize all the gifts residing in you, but when you are truly anointed, you don't have to promote yourself.

God didn't reveal who Jesus was until He was thirty. You are about to turn thirty because God is getting ready to show the world who you really are. People have ignored you because they didn't think you were special. They made over other people who didn't have half your talent, but God noticed your faithfulness. In one day God is going to show the world who you are. Your waiting was not wasted time; the wait was God's requirement, so that when you're introduced to the world, you will be ready.

At the Jordan, God will show you who you really are. You are more than what you think you are. You are more than your parents' offspring, the drama of your past, or the abuse, neglect, and hurt you've gone through. You are more than your last experience.

This is your Jordan, and God is about to show you who you really are: A child of God. If you don't know who you are, you may miss God's introduction because you won't even think He is talking about you. That is why so many of us miss our cue and come onto the stage late. God has already called our name, but we didn't know He was talking about us, because we've bought into what other people have said about us. We have taken on the identity given to us by other people. Other people call us stupid, ugly, crazy, but God calls us Beloved. If God called your name, would you be able to answer? Could you believe He is talking about you?

AFFIRMATION

What brings pleasure to the Father? Was it Jesus' obedience, submission, and humility? Of course the answer is yes, but all of that is just another way of saying that by going to the Jordan, Jesus moved into His destiny and found His purpose. We bring glory to God when we walk in our purpose.

Some people say that God doesn't want us to be successful; He wants us to be faithful. But I have recently discovered that God doesn't mind if I'm both. I *can* have it all. Jesus said, "I brought glory to your Name by doing what you told me to do." Is your life bringing glory to God? Are you doing what God has told you to do?

We have to examine ourselves, know who we are, and fulfill our purpose. I started out with fifty members. If I had died with fifty members—while God gave me seed for thousands of members—God would not have gotten the glory, no matter how faithfully I served. God would have looked at me and said, "You wicked and lazy person; I put thousands in you and you bring me fifty?" If I have seed for thousands and I'm too lazy to work, nurture, pray, fast, cast vision, lead, and produce, then I am a failure. However, if all God required of me is fifty and that is what I bring Him, He would say, "Well done, good and faithful servant."

Some of you reading this are anointed with many gifts and talents. You're making money for someone else while God has put a business inside of you. You are not bringing God glory by holding down a job, even if you do pay tithes and give offerings. If God has put a business in you and you are working for someone else, you are not bringing Him glory. If God made you a teacher and you would rather work in a factory because you make more money, you are a failure. If you are doing anything other than your assignment, you are a failure regardless of how successful you are. The song inside your heart, the book you need to write, and the play you need to create will remain undone until you step out and do what God has told you to do. God has kept some of you alive to give you another chance to complete your assignment.

If God called you in for an interim report, would He be pleased? If God called for a meeting to see what you are producing with the gifts He has given you, would He be pleased? Most of us are not even close to doing what He has told us to do because of fear, timidity, and uncertainty; we often lack confidence in our ability to do what God has called us to do. You need to be obedient to the calling not only because God expects you to obey, but also because once you do it, no one will ever be able to say you're a failure and it can't be done.

ACCEPTANCE

There are three things Jesus accepted in the Jordan: The Holy Spirit, the Father's approval, and the Spirit's leading. The Jordan is also the place where we accept the keys to a meaningful life:

- Power. We know that the Holy Spirit is power, so the first thing Jesus received at the Jordan was power: "And, lo, the heavens were opened unto him, and he saw the Spirit of God descending like a dove, and lighting upon him" (Matthew 3:16, KJV). If we are going to live victorious, productive lives we need power, too. If we are going to live the life God wants us to live—whether it's writing, singing, preaching, teaching, starting a business, or whatever—we need power beyond our own limited abilities.

- Praise. I don't mean shouting praise or giving God praise. Jesus received praise from the Father: "And lo a voice from heaven, saying, This is my beloved Son, in whom I am well pleased" (Matthew 3:17, KJV). Isn't that a key to meaningful life? Everybody wants someone to praise them; to tell them they did a good job. Many of us are starved for positive affirmation. We want our spouses, children, co-workers, friends, and family to praise us. We also want God to praise us. I don't want to work this hard and not hear Him say, "Well done." It matters that He praises me. I want my wife to say I am a good husband and my children to say I am a good father; but I also want to hear God say, "Well done." Don't be afraid of praise. The Father loves to lavish praise on us. He wants to say, "Well done" to us.

- Purpose. The Spirit led Jesus to the wilderness where He discovered His purpose. If we want to live a meaningful life, we, too, must find our purpose: "Then was Jesus led up of the Spirit into the wilderness to be tempted of the devil" (Matthew 4:1, KJV). Stop doing what everybody says you should do and do what God has called you to do. People may look at you like you have two heads and talk about you like a dog; they may criticize you, ostracize you, and push you to the edge, but it will be worth it. Give people something to talk about by doing what God has called you to do. You are not ready for your destiny or purpose until you don't mind that people are talking about you, acting funny, or treating you differently. Keep your eyes on the prize, stay focused on the vision, and trust God to bring you through.

You must go to Jordan, for it is your place of acknowledgement. Jesus was thirty years old when He first heard the Father publicly acknowledge Him. The incident in the temple when Jesus was twelve was not God's perfect will. I am not saying that Jesus was disobedient, because He is perfect in obedience; but I am saying the fact that God never said anything simply means that it wasn't the time for Jesus to be revealed. You can't rush God. So, many of you wonder when is it going to be your turn; and the answer is only when you get to the Jordan, settle the issue of who you are, and embrace what you have to do.

The Jordan is the place of affirmation where God lets you know He is pleased with you. The Jordan becomes our blessed place because it is where we find the reason we were born.

CHAPTER NINETEEN

—

The Wilderness:
The Place Where It's Just God and You

Every now and then God allows painful things to happen to us, so that once we get on the other side of the issue, we can help someone else. This is why we shouldn't be so quick to ask God to get us out of trouble. Instead of asking God to get us out, we should ask God to take us through. When we go through something, we get the benefit of the experience. If God brought us out of everything, we would have nothing to shout about. The things that cause us to praise God the most are the things that God has brought us through.

When Jesus was baptized at the Jordan, God acknowledged Him as His Son. After being baptized, Jesus was led into the wilderness to be tempted by the devil. You may never have a Jordan River experience, but you will have a wilderness experience. The wilderness becomes the fifth place Jesus turned into a blessed place.

God seems to enjoy the process of taking us to the desert after great moments of inspiration and revelation. Everything that goes wrong in your life is not the devil; sometimes the adverse thing is God working on us, because He knows that the wilderness is a necessity. The Apostle Paul tells us of two times it happened to him.

The first time was after Paul's conversion on the Damascus Road:

> "But then something happened! For it pleased God in His kindness to choose me and call me, even before I was born! What undeserved mercy! Then He revealed His Son to me so that I could proclaim the Good News about Jesus to the Gentiles. When all this happened to me, I did not rush out to consult with anyone else; nor did I go up to Jerusalem to consult with those who were apostles before I was. No, I went away into Arabia and later returned to the city of Damascus." (Galatians 1:15-17, NLT)

The second time was when Paul was shown a glimpse of the third heaven:

> "This boasting is all so foolish, but let me go on. Let me tell about the visions and revelations I received from the Lord. I was caught up into the third heaven fourteen years ago. Whether my body was there or just my spirit, I don't know, only God knows. But I do know that I was caught up into paradise and heard things so astounding that they cannot be told. That experience is something worth boasting about, but I am not going to do it. I am going to boast only about my weaknesses. I have plenty to boast about and would be no fool

in doing it, because I would be telling the truth.
But I won't do it. I don't want anyone to think
more highly of me than what they can actually
see in my life and my message, even though I
have received wonderful revelations from God.
But to keep me from getting puffed up, I was
given a thorn in my flesh, a messenger from Satan
to torment me and keep me from getting proud."
(2 Corinthians 12:1-7, NLT)

There are some things we will only learn in the wilderness. Jesus
shows us how to turn our wilderness into a blessed place.

The wilderness is a place of teaching

We are told that Jesus was led by the Spirit into the wilderness to
be tempted by the devil:

Immediately the Holy Spirit compelled Jesus to
go into the wilderness. He was there for forty
days, being tempted by Satan. He was out among
the wild animals, and angels took care of him.
(Mark 1:12-13, NLT)

Anytime you are in school there are always tests somewhere in
the curriculum to determine how much you have learned and
retained. Jesus' wilderness challenges taught Him how to trust
God for everything. One of the ways our wilderness becomes
blessed is by learning to rely only on God, because the wilderness
is where God delivers us from counting on and depending on
people. We realize that our lives are in God's hands.

The wilderness is a place of training

Jesus can identify with every temptation we will ever face:

> "Seeing then that we have a great High Priest who
> has passed through the heavens, Jesus the Son of
> God, let us hold fast our confession." (Hebrews
> 4:14, NKJV)

The temptation in the wilderness allowed Jesus to identify with us and the temptations we encounter, and that is the kind of Savior we need. Because Jesus can relate to us, He is then able to intercede on our behalf. When we stumble and have to ask God for mercy, Jesus is there pleading our case:

> "Therefore, he is able to save completely those who
> come to God through him, because he always
> lives to intercede for them." (Hebrews 7:25)

When I go to God and ask for help before I sin, Jesus is able to tell God, "I know what he is going through because I have been there." If I need forgiveness after I have sinned, Jesus tells God, "I was wounded for their transgressions, bruised for their iniquities, hung up for their hang ups, and died for their sin."

Jesus went through the wilderness so that He could intercede and impart strength to us. We love Him identifying and interceding, but in our moments of weakness, we need Him to impart strength so we can stand and resist the temptations.

The wilderness is a place of triumph

One Friday on the outskirts of Jerusalem, men took our Lord and made Him carry a cross down the Via Dolorosa; they nailed Him to an old rugged cross, and dropped it in the ground. They hung

Him high and stretched Him wide. He cried, "It is finished," and died until death died. The fight was won on Calvary. In the battle with Satan, Jesus emerged victorious.

God didn't send Jesus into the wilderness to lose, but to win. Even though the fight is already over, you still have to show up and go through the wilderness.

COMING OUT OF THE WILDERNESS

There are some life moments that stand out so dramatically that we are never the same:

> Jesus returned to Galilee in the power of the Spirit, and news about Him spread through the whole countryside. (Luke 4:14)

Years ago I had a conversation with the late Dr. Evans Bromley Marshall, who led the Lafayette Avenue Church of God in Brooklyn, New York, for over fifty years. Dr. Marshall shared with me insight about the above passage and said, "Do you notice this is the first time the Bible refers to Jesus being filled with the Holy Spirit? When he was baptized, the Spirit landed on Him in the form of a dove; but this passage said that when He came out of the wilderness, it was in the power of the Spirit. Now, if Jesus needed the Holy Ghost, what about you and me?" Dr. Marshall asked me that question almost forty years ago and it has never left my mind. The question always reminds me of the importance of being filled with the Person and Power of the Holy Spirit. We all need to be filled with the Spirit if we are going to serve God, because the Holy Spirit can take us where our ability would never get us.

God controls the timing of our tests and never allows the next test to come before we are prepared for it. God knows what we can handle and when. And even when we are going through, God has timed our tests to come when we can best handle them.

The night my mother called to say the doctors found a lump in her breast and that they were going to do exploratory surgery, I went for a walk and started talking to God: "You are God and can do whatever you want to, but I am not ready for my mother to die. I can't handle it now. I can't take it now. I'm asking you to give her and me some more time." That was in 1986. My mother died in February of 1988. When they called to tell me she had slipped into a coma, the Lord said to me, "You had time to get ready. I am not raising her up or bringing her back, but I didn't take her in 1986 because you asked me to give you time. This is the time and I am going to take her. You are going to go through this and be able to stand; you are not going to fall apart. I have taken you through enough, I have taught you enough, and I have shown you enough, so you can handle this." It hurt me when my mother died, but I didn't fall apart because God knows my frame, He remembers that we are dust, and knows how much we can bear.

God's tests are not permanent. No matter what you're going through, remember, it is just a test. You may feel like you have been going through forever, but your test is not permanent. You have been in the storm so long that it seems like it has become your permanent address, but in God's time He will bring you out.

Jesus came out of the wilderness in the power of the Spirit— drenched and saturated—and with the Spirit at work in and through Him. I can't help but wonder how much power Jesus would have had if He had not gone into the wilderness. There is a crisis we must go through before we are filled with the Spirit. There has to be surrender and sacrifice, a yielding that allows the Holy Spirit to take up residence in us and to work through us. There are a lot of people who think they are filled but they aren't, because there hasn't been a yielding. You have to sacrifice and if it doesn't hurt, you haven't put it on the altar.

The wilderness became a blessed place for Jesus because of what happened while He was there. And when He came out of the wilderness, He was changed.

Jesus came out of the wilderness anointed

> "The Spirit of the Lord is on me, because He has
> anointed me to preach good news to the poor. He
> has sent me to proclaim freedom for the prison-
> ers and recovery of sight for the blind, to release
> the oppressed, to proclaim the year of the Lord's
> favor." (Luke 4:18-19)

The anointing is an impartation of power, and it doesn't come
cheap. That is why most people would rather operate in the
flesh because it's easier. To stay under the anointing requires a
daily payment. The anointing is about walking and operating
in power every day, not just on Saturday night before Sunday
morning. The anointing allows you to fulfill your assignment
and purpose:

- When you're anointed, you can do whatever God has for
  you to do.

- When you're anointed, you can do whatever God has for
  you to do, *and* you can do it well.

- When you're anointed, you can do whatever God has
  for you to do, you can do it well, *and* you can do it with
  ease.

Jesus came out of the wilderness with authority

The word *authority* means you have been empowered to do what
you do:

> He went to Nazareth, where He had been brought
> up, and on the Sabbath day He went into the

> synagogue, as was His custom. And He stood
> up to read. The scroll of the prophet Isaiah was
> handed to Him. Unrolling it, He found the place
> where it is written. . . (Luke 4:16-17)

Another word for anointing could be deputized, which means
you have been sent and sanctioned. When I am functioning in
my anointing, I have authority that gives me courage, confidence,
and covering. The reason a five foot, five inch female highway
patrol officer can stand on the highway and pull over an eighteen
wheel truck is because of who is backing her up: the laws of the
state and nation. When she does her job, it's not just her, but who
she represents. When you tell the devil to back up, it's not just
you talking but who is backing you up: The Father, the Son, and
the Holy Ghost!

<u>Jesus came out of the wilderness ready for action</u>

Jesus had the anointing and the authority, but He knew it wouldn't
mean anything without action:

> Then He rolled up the scroll, gave it back to the
> attendant and sat down. The eyes of everyone in
> the synagogue were fastened on Him, and He
> began by saying to them, "Today, this Scripture is
> fulfilled in your hearing." (Luke 4:20-21)

We are not anointed to brag, strut around, and hold court
among ourselves. We are not anointed to sit in the sanctuary to
compare ourselves among ourselves, or to brag about our own
self-righteousness. We are anointed and given authority to do
something for God. People are dying and God needs somebody
to get them. Teenagers have no hope for a future and God needs

somebody to get them. Senior saints feel unloved and unwanted and God needs somebody to get them.

Jesus came out of the wilderness with anointing, authority, and action and you can too when you follow His example of turning the wilderness into a blessed place.

CHAPTER TWENTY

—

Gethsemane:

The Place Where You

Learn To Say "Yes"

God has a place that He has physically, spiritually, and emotionally prepared for us; and once we find it, that place becomes our blessed place. The blessed place is not just a geographical location; it is a place of optimal living and experience. It is the place where we discover our destiny and purpose, the reason for which we were born.

The sixth place Jesus turned into the blessed place is the Garden of Gethsemane, the place of crushing. The word *Gethsemane* means oil press. The Garden was the place where olives were taken to be crushed, so that the oil inside would be released. When God wants to get something out of us, He sends us to Gethsemane where we are crushed and bruised; not so we can be destroyed, but so that what is inside of us will be released.

We often run from Gethsemane because of what it means; but in doing so, we miss what it produces. If there is no Gethsemane, then there is no oil. Just like a rose must be crushed to produce its fragrance, an olive must be crushed to produce oil. An olive that looks pretty and undamaged still has the oil inside. The only way to get the oil from the inside of an olive is to beat it up. It is the same with us. When we walk around without scars or bruises and no pain in our lives, we look good, but we are shallow. We don't have a testimony and we can't help anyone else. After being on the oil press in Gethsemane, we look different and have a testimony, because Gethsemane was created to bring out the best from inside us:

> Then Jesus went with his disciples to a place called Gethsemane, and he said to them, "Sit here while I go over there and pray." (Matthew 26:36)

We are told that on a particular night in Jesus' life—His last night on earth before going to the cross—He retreated to Gethsemane. This is important because Gethsemane was a familiar place to Jesus; He had been there before, which is how He was able to survive. This was not the first time Jesus had been in a place where He had to depend on God.

Gethsemane was a distant place away from the city and the crowds. Thank God for friends and family, but every now and then, you need to be alone. God will take you through some things where no one can walk with you; the only way you will make it is to be alone with God in Gethsemane.

Gethsemane was also a quiet place. We live in a culture that is noise-obsessed. Even some of our churches are that way. All worship is not loud; sometimes we need to sit in the presence of God in blessed quietness to allow for reflection, meditation, and introspection. We don't want to get quiet, because we don't want to be alone with our thoughts.

It was in Gethsemane that Jesus struggled to get to the will of God. All of us will and must have a Gethsemane. The quality of your Christian experience is suspect if there are no Gethsemanes dotting the landscape of your journey.

GETHSEMANE IS A PLACE OF STRUGGLE

Gethsemane wasn't about Jesus not wanting to do the will of God; it was about Jesus bringing His flesh to the level of His desire:

> He took Peter and the two sons of Zebedee along with Him, and He began to be sorrowful and troubled. Then He said to them, "My soul is overwhelmed with sorrow to the point of death. Stay here and keep watch with me." Going a little farther, He fell with His face to the ground and prayed, "My Father, if it is possible, may this cup be taken from me. Yet not as I will, but as you will." (Matthew 26:37-39)

It was impossible for Jesus not to want to do the will of God, because He is a Son—perfect in obedience. However, His flesh was another matter. Jesus is totally human in this story, and although committed to doing the Father's will, His flesh was resisting. We go through the same thing; our head and heart want to do right, but getting the rest of our body to line up is another story.

This is why Jesus had compassion on the disciples when He came back and found them asleep. Rather than get upset, Jesus understood: "Watch and pray, lest you enter into temptation. The spirit indeed is willing, but the flesh is weak" (Matthew 26:41, NKJV). While the disciples were fighting sleep Jesus was in the garden fighting His flesh; and He understood that they were having as much of a struggle as He was. That is why He had compassion on Peter when he denied Him because He understood the battle between flesh and will (John 18:15-27). Thank God we have a Savior who understands our struggle.

GETHSEMANE IS A PLACE OF SUBMISSION

After praying for a while, Jesus made a shift from struggle to submission:

> "My Father, if it is not possible for this cup to be taken away unless I drink it, may your will be done." (Matthew 26:42)

There is a difference between submission and surrender. Jesus doesn't surrender, He submits. In most cases surrender occurs under duress. Surrender comes because we are made to; submission comes because we want to. Submission is not surrender. We don't surrender because God broke our arm and made us; we submit because we love Him and want to be aligned with Him. It is a voluntary act.

When you get married, the vows don't say surrender to one another, although that word would most likely describe what goes on in most marital relationships because of the conflict. The biblical paradigm is not surrender, but submission to one another. There is a pattern of love, trust, and faith. When you know you are loved, that you can trust the other person, and have faith to know that they are going to be there, submission is not a problem.

Jesus submitted to God at Gethsemane because His faith, love, and trust were complete.

GETHSEMANE IS A PLACE OF STRENGTH

Having struggled through to submission, Jesus found new strength:

> Then He returned to the disciples and said to them, "Are you still sleeping and resting? Look, the hour is near, and the Son of Man is betrayed

into the hands of sinners. Rise, let us go! Here comes my betrayer!" (Matthew 26:45-46)

Jesus had prayed His way through to submission and gained strength to handle whatever was coming:

> While he was still speaking, Judas, one of the Twelve, arrived. With him was a large crowd armed with swords and clubs, sent from the chief priests and the elders of the people. Now the betrayer had arranged a signal with them: "The one I kiss is the man; arrest him." Going at once to Jesus, Judas said, "Greetings, Rabbi!" and kissed him. Jesus replied, "Friend, do what you came for." Then the men stepped forward, seized Jesus and arrested him. With that, one of Jesus' companions reached for his sword, drew it out and struck the servant of the high priest, cutting off his ear. "Put your sword back in its place," Jesus said to him, "for all who draw the sword will die by the sword. Do you think I cannot call on my Father, and he will at once put at my disposal more than twelve legions of angels? But how then would the Scriptures be fulfilled that say it must happen in this way?" (Matthew 26:47-54)

With new strength you can face whatever life brings your way. I know things aren't perfect in your life, but you are still alive. And God will give you strength to handle what is ahead when you allow Him to turn your Gethsemane into the blessed place.

CHAPTER TWENTY-ONE

—

Calvary: The Place of Completion

Do you know why you were born? The reason I ask is because I am convinced that the answer holds the key to our destiny and purpose. Until we find out why we are here, we can never experience life in all of its fullness. When we look at Jesus, we see a man who knew who He was and why He was born. He knew the reason for His existence:

> Then Pilate entered the Praetorium again, called Jesus, and said to Him, "Are You the King of the Jews?" Jesus answered him, "Are you speaking for yourself about this, or did others tell you this concerning Me?" Pilate answered, "Am I a Jew? Your own nation and the chief priests have delivered You to me. What have You done?" Jesus answered, "My kingdom is not of this world. If My kingdom were of this world, My servants would fight, so that I should not be delivered to the Jews; but now My kingdom is not from here." Pilate therefore said to Him, "Are You a king then?" Jesus answered, "You say rightly that I am

a king. For this cause I was born, and for this cause I have come into the world, that I should bear witness to the truth. Everyone who is of the truth hears My voice." Pilate said to Him, "What is truth?" (John 18:33-38, NKJV)

Knowing your purpose will help you protect your time. As we grow older we look back on the years that we have squandered because we didn't know the reason for our existence. Think of all the years you have let slip through your fingers. Don't waste your time; don't allow life to steal your most precious commodity. None of us know how much time we have left.

Knowing your purpose will help you know who you are and why you are here; you don't have to pretend to be someone else. You don't have to do things that you are neither anointed nor called to do just because somebody says you should. One of the greatest feelings in the world is to wake up and go to the place of employment that is your calling.

Knowing your purpose also keeps you from getting sidetracked. When you know your purpose, you know to say no to things that are not part of your agenda. Successful people know when to say no. That doesn't mean that other things aren't important or don't need to be done; they just don't need to be done by them. Don't get sidetracked by negative, critical people who want to tell you what they think you need to be doing. Find out what you are here to accomplish and stay true to what God has called you to do.

The Greek poet Homer wrote an epic that includes a tale about the Sirens, whose beautiful song caused sailors to wreck their ships on the rocky shore near their island. Odysseus was determined to get his ship past the Sirens and to make it to his destination; he covered the sailors' ears with beeswax so they wouldn't hear the call. He wanted them to turn a deaf ear so they would stay on course. We need to embrace that concept. Turn a deaf ear to people who tell you what you can't do; don't get sidetracked by them.

When we find our purpose, we do not have to compete, compromise, or compare. We are not fighting against each other. We don't have to compromise our standards in order to make people like us. We don't have to compare ourselves to anyone else because we are unique.

"Pilate therefore said to Him, 'Are You a king then?' Jesus answered, 'You say rightly that I am a king'" (John 18:37(a), NKJV). Jesus stood before Pilate with confidence because He knew who He was. Jesus went to Calvary—the seventh place He turned into the blessed place—with confidence knowing that it was the Father's will. Each of us has a Calvary we must experience, because Calvary is crucial to getting to the blessed place. Calvary is the place where we willingly die. It is the place where we lay down our lives. For Jesus it was on a Friday on the outskirts of Jerusalem, on a hill called Golgotha, where He gave His life—one time for the sins of the world. For us it is dying to ourselves. God daily demands that we make another payment on our Calvary—we forgive people who have done us wrong; we go the extra mile and turn the other cheek; we are nice to people who are nasty to us; we pray for people who misuse us—we live out Calvary every day.

CALVARY IS WHERE YOU FACE YOUR FOES

The mob gathered around Jesus and jeered Him; yet, He was able to pray and ask God to forgive them. The power of Calvary takes your enemies' power. For three and a half years, Jesus' enemies had harassed Him everywhere He traveled, always trying to catch Him doing something they could use to condemn Him. At Calvary they did their worst and thought they had won. They didn't understand. . .they had lost. After Jesus went to Calvary, there was nothing else His enemies could do to Him.

The same is true for us. If your worst enemy died and the funeral home allowed you twenty minutes to do whatever you wanted to do to the body, the person would still be dead and unable to feel anything you were doing, Dead is dead, even if you smack, stab, or shoot the corpse. That's good news for us (not that you want to deface a corpse) because it means that the devil can't hurt us. We are walking dead people and there is nothing our enemies can do to us:

> "I have been crucified with Christ and I no longer live, but Christ lives in me. The life I now live in the body, I live by faith in the Son of God, who loved me and gave himself for me." (Galatians 2:20)

Once we come to Jesus, we die to ourselves. God takes us to Calvary because it is where we face our foes.

CALVARY IS WHERE WE FIGHT PAST THE PAIN

Crucifixion was the most horrendous death ever devised by man. Yet, Jesus would not take anything to deaden the pain because He knew that He had to feel everything. He still had unfinished business:

> One of the criminals who hung there hurled insults at him: "Aren't you the Christ? Save yourself and us!" But the other criminal rebuked him. "Don't you fear God," he said, "since you are under the same sentence? We are punished justly, for we are getting what our deeds deserve. But this man has done nothing wrong." Then he said, "Jesus, remember me when you come into your kingdom." Jesus answered him, "I tell you

the truth, today you will be with me in paradise."
(Luke 23:39-43)

Have you ever pushed past the pain to do what God wanted you to do? I'm not just talking about physical pain, but emotional, spiritual, relational pain. Have you been able to push past the pain because there was still work for you to do? You have to endure the pain, but God will give you more grace and help you fight past your pain to get the blessings of Calvary.

Pregnant women know how to push past the pain. When it's time for delivery, the doctor tells them to push even though pushing causes pain. Every time they push there are more contractions and pain and they feel like their pelvic area is about to explode; but they can't stop pushing. The only way to get life out is to push. The only way to create something new is to push. The only way to produce a new work is to push. The only way to go to the next level is to push past the pain. So PUSH!

CALVARY HELPS US FINISH OUR ASSIGNMENT

On the cross, Jesus cried out with a loud voice and then shouted, "It is finished!" Notice He didn't say, "I am finished." There is a big difference between "it" and "I."

This is where the saints get confused. We personalize our struggles and problems and make that our pain. The problem is in our life, but it isn't our life. We are not our struggle and we are more than our dilemma. You have a drinking problem so the world says you're an alcoholic. You have a drug problem so the world says you're a drug addict. You have a sexual obsession so the world says you're a deviant. The world's psychology teaches us to personalize and embody our neurosis, instead of teaching us to say we are a creature of God with a problem. We are not the problem, because God made us and made us good. Sin creates chaos in us, but we have to separate ourselves from the struggle. We might have a problem or a habit, but Jesus is the Problem Solver and the Habit Breaker.

So what was finished? Jesus' mission, work, pain, suffering, and separation from His Father. It was all finished. After the grief comes the glory:

> For his anger endureth but a moment; in his favour is life: weeping may endure for a night, but joy cometh in the morning. (Psalm 30:5, KJV)

Jesus endured the cross, despising the shame but keeping His eyes on the prize. He was looking for that which was ahead. The joy that was awaiting Him gave Him the power to handle what He was temporarily going through.

Lift your eyes above where you are and see the joy of what is coming. It will help you handle what you are currently going through. If you could only see how you will look when you come out of this; if you could only see what you are going to have after you have gone through this; if you could only see where God is going to take you after you have endured this, you would begin giving God praise right now!

Calvary will help you finish your assignment. This is the place where it is finished! Your season of pain and suffering is finished. Your time of lack and poverty is finished. Today is the start of a new era in your life; not just a new day, but a new season. Push one more time. You are about to give birth to your destiny.

CONCLUSION
THE COST OF LIVING JUST WENT UP

When I was in public school, I had a teacher named David Stern, who taught me as much out of the classroom as he did in it. Mr. Stern believed in me when I sometimes didn't believe in myself, and he was concerned that I not waste and squander the gifts, skills, and abilities that God had given me. Mr. Stern often talked with me about what I was going to do with my life, and one day he made a statement that I have never forgotten: "Timothy, always remember that with gifts and callings come responsibility. When God gives you something that you didn't earn, merit, or deserve, you have a responsibility to use it, cultivate it, and share it so others are blessed by it." Mr. Stern told me that I was blessed, gifted, and talented, and that I didn't have the right to waste it because it wasn't given to me just for me; it was given to me for others. Another way of saying that is, "For everyone to whom much is given, from him much will be required" (Luke 12:48, NKJV).

We have been greatly blessed by God and we don't have the option of wasting what God has given to us. We have been called into the Kingdom for such a time as this. In other words, you can't be gifted without responsibility, and you can't be blessed without God expecting more from you.

When people ask me to pray for God to bless them, I sometimes wonder if that is really what they want me to do. Blessings don't come for you to be able to brag, boast, or strut around. God blesses us to put in circulation what already belongs to Him. Do you understand that everything in the world belongs to God—not just your money, but your time, talent, and treasure? Everything we have belongs to God and should be given back to God, so He can bless others through what He has given us. If you are called to sing, then sing with the right spirit, not to be seen, but to be a blessing. If you are called to preach, you should not preach for reputation, but to be a blessing. If you are called to teach, don't teach so that you will be seen as brilliant, smart, witty and engaging, but so that you will be a blessing. If God has blessed you financially, you are not to brag about what you have given and who you have helped, but you are to quietly be a blessing to others because the Bible says, "Your Father who sees what is done in secret, will reward you" (Matthew 6:18). You don't do things for the approval of people; you do them for the glory of God and He will repay you.

There is a price for being blessed. The more blessed you are, the greater your price is going to be. There is a price for living in the place of blessing. There are a lot of us who get to a blessed place, but lose our position because we don't want to constantly and continuously pay the price. Having achieved something, you must be willing to pay the price to stay in the blessed place. When you get blessed, you can't sit back and become spiritually fat, out of shape, and expect to keep winning spiritual victories. You have an adversary who wants to steal your crown. The only way to hold onto your crown is to stay in training, so you can win the fight. Every time you bend your knees, you are in training. Every time you read your Bible, you are in training. Every time you raise your hands to praise God, you are in training. Every time you shout and give God praise, you are in training. The longer you stay in training, the stronger you will be and the better you will hold onto what God has given you. When God blesses us, we must assume the responsibility associated with the blessing:

- We must not squander the blessing, so we need wisdom.

- We must not hoard our blessing, because it was given for us to bless others. We are to be conduits, not vaults.

- We must not devalue the blessing, in that we must recognize, appreciate, and guard what has been given to us.

This responsibility requires discipline, discernment, and diligence, which come into our lives as we exercise the spiritual principles of supplication, study, stewardship, staying in the Word, praying, and giving.

Living in the Blessed Place is more than an accumulation of material things. It is an attitude of gratitude for all that God has done.